CONTENTS

ANCIENT ROME
IN FIVE MINUTES

Rome was not built in a day. All roads lead to Rome. When in Rome do as the Romans do. There is an element of truth in all three of these common English expressions, as we shall find out in the course of this book.

The history of ancient Rome is the history of a city, of its people, and of its empire, which, at its height, encompassed all the lands around the Mediterranean Sea and stretched from Britain in the west to Syria in the east. Rome's history is no longer seen in terms of its rise, decline and fall but rather as a dynamic and extended process of adaption and transition in relation to changing economic and political circumstances over the centuries. Roman culture and civilization was reliant on the wealth created by war and conquest and dependent on slavery. While much of its history can be understood through examining the biographies of its emperors, more still about Rome can be gleaned from looking at the lives of its ordinary citizens and from the archaeological exploration of the very fabric of the city: its forum and other civic spaces, monuments and statues, its streets, bridges, aqueducts, temples, shops and bars, apartment blocks, houses and tombs.

In this book we will consider the physical setting of the city and discuss how this natural geography and topography affected its development. We will examine the myths and historical truths about the founding of Rome – literally the city of Romulus – and the city's early years and explore the bloody transition of Rome from the rule of kings to a republic and more bloodily still from republic to empire. We will look at the lives of its most famous, and most infamous, emperors and examine the tumultuous and complex events which led to the end of the Roman Empire. Pressures on the frontiers and mass migrations of barbarian peoples in the fourth and fifth centuries AD represent just part of the historical narrative of this time. Great attention will also be paid to reconstructing the daily lives, culture and beliefs of the ordinary people of Rome. Provincial life in Roman Britain will also briefly be considered. We will attempt to explore the plethora of Roman beliefs, ritual customs and religions, and examine the pagan world of

Opposite: Marcus Aurelius riding in a triumphal chariot. (Capitoline Museums, Rome)

The Roman Forum.

gods that would, as the fourth century AD progressed, change and make way for a Christian god. Finally we will look at the Romans in death, questioning their beliefs in an afterlife, looking at their burial rites, and discussing the nature of their commemorative funerary monuments, including the most unusual pyramid tomb of Gaius Cestius and the equally unique tomb of Eurysaces the Baker.

The lives and achievements of a number of individual Romans such as these will be considered throughout the book. Almost inevitably, however, most of these individuals will be emperors or other members of the imperial household such as generals and politicians – the powerful members of Roman society. When exploring a male-dominated society such as ancient Rome it is also important to seek out the stories of women, and I have consciously aspired to do this throughout the book. Wherever possible I have also tried to introduce some detail about individual Romans of the lower classes, so, for instance, while you will read about the emperors Augustus and Constantine you will also learn a little about Vitalis the pork butcher, Priscus and Verus the gladiators, Carpophores the beast slayer from the arena, Diocles the charioteer, the lesbian freedwomen Fonteia Helena and Fonteia Eleusis, and the anonymous slave of the master Pascasius whose collar tag has been found by archaeologists.

The people of Rome at different times in their lives laughed and cried, hoped and feared, lusted or loved as much as we do today. Emotions such as these are universal among humans and are not historically bound in any way. However, the Romans were otherwise not 'just like us', and historical approaches which resurrect this old saw are seldom insightful. In the same vein, to view the Roman world through the self-absorbed prism of 'what did the Romans ever do for us?' is equally as self-defeating and usually as uninformative. I never cease to be amazed at just how strange Roman society was in many ways and how it can never fully be understood or interpreted by us for that very reason. That is not to say that we cannot try, but in order to do so we need to muster both historical and archaeological evidence and adopt an almost anthropological approach to the study of this dead society and its culture.

The idea that Rome's history was somehow unreservedly 'glorious' and that the creation of its empire provided a positive parallel to the British empire was a Victorian interpretation that holds no sway nowadays. Indeed, if we are to learn lessons from Roman history they are not always palatable truths. Therefore in this book we will also discuss the harsh realities of Roman slavery, the savagery and bloody spectacle of gladiatorial combat and the almost unbelievably cruel treatment of animals slaughtered for entertainment in the arena, as religious sacrifices and sometimes in ancient festival rites. We cannot make a simple judgement on a people as complex in behaviours and beliefs as the ancient Romans; we can only try to interpret their culture as far as is possible at such a great remove.

The timespan covered in this book is considerable, the narrative beginning with events in 753 BC and ending with the deposing of the last Western emperor, Romulus Augustulus, in AD 476, representing a period of around 1,200 years. The settlement supposedly founded by the mythological Romulus was a very different place from the 'city of brick' turned into 'a city of marble' and ruled over by the first emperor, Augustus. Equally, this marble city was vastly different in appearance and character from the city set on the road of transformation from a pagan city to a Christian city under the fourth-century emperor Constantine. Over the centuries, while so much in Rome remained the same, yet more still changed.

While the opportunity to enjoy Rome on the equivalent of ten *denarii* a day is long gone, it is hoped that this book might inspire you to visit the city some time and to explore its many extant monuments and its numerous museums. Or you might choose to stay at home and discover more about ancient Rome through following up the further reading suggested at the end of this book or by visiting some of the recommended websites online. Whatever your choice, *bona fortuna*, or 'good luck', as the Romans would have wished you.

TIMELINE

c. 753 BC
Founding of Rome by Romulus

753–510 BC
Reign of the five kings

c. 600 BC
The digging of the great sewer, the *Cloaca Maxima*

510–509 BC
Overthrow of the last king, Tarquinius Superbus, and founding of the Roman Republic

387 BC
Sacking of Rome by Gauls under Brennus

386 BC
Founding of the river port of Ostia

312 BC
The building of the first aqueduct, the *Aqua Appia*

264 BC
The first gladiatorial contests take place as funerary games

264–146 BC
The Punic Wars against Carthage

133–121 BC
Plebeian agitation supported by the Gracchi brothers

88–82 BC
Struggle for power between Marius and Sulla

70s BC
The Spartacus uprising of slaves

58–49 BC
Caesar's conquest of Gaul

55–54 BC
Expeditions to Britain

49–45 BC
The First Triumvirate and struggle for power between Pompey the Great, Crassus and Julius Caesar

44 BC
The assassination of Julius Caesar

44–31 BC
Civil war between Octavian (Augustus) and Antony

31 BC
The Battle of Actium and the end of the Roman Republic

c. 30 BC
Building of the Tomb of Eurysaces the Baker

31 BC–AD 14
Reign of Augustus, first emperor of Rome

c. 12 BC
Building of the Pyramid of Cestius

AD 29
Death of Livia, first empress of Rome and mother of Tiberius

AD 43
The conquest of Britain by Claudius

AD 46
Foundation of deep-water port at Portus under Claudius

AD 54–68
Reign of Nero

AD 60
Boudiccan uprising in Britain

AD 64
Great fire in Rome

AD 80
Inaugural games at the Colosseum

AD 96–180
Reigns of 'the good emperors': Nerva, Trajan, Hadrian, Antoninus Pius, Marcus Aurelius

AD 124
The building of Hadrian's Wall in Britain

AD 180–192
Reign of Commodus

AD 271–275
The building of the Servian Wall in Rome

AD 293–313
The Tetrarchy, or rule of four emperors

AD 301
Diocletian's Edict on Maximum Prices

AD 306–337
Reign of Constantine the Great

AD 312
Battle of the Milvian Bridge

AD 313
Edict of Milan on religious tolerance

AD 330
Founding of Constantinople, the 'New Rome'

AD 357
Roman victory at the Battle of Strasbourg

AD 378
Roman defeat at the Battle of Adrianople

AD 408
Arrest and execution of Stilicho

AD 410
The sacking of Rome by the Visigoths and the ending of Roman Britain as a province

AD 439
The Vandals capture Carthage

AD 444–453
Threats to Roman Empire from Huns led by Attila

AD 454
The sacking of Rome by the Vandals

AD 468
Romans fail to retake former north African provinces

AD 476
Deposing of Romulus Augustulus, last emperor of the Roman west

The Capitoline wolf bronze statue. Figures of Romulus and Remus added later. (Capitoline Museum, Rome)

1

THE FOUNDING OF ROME: MYTH AND HISTORY, THE GEOGRAPHY OF THE CITY

The city of Rome was not actually built in a day, but it is possible that we can assign its official or legal foundation date to a specific day, 21 April 753 BC, or so some archaeologists and ancient historians would argue. Whatever the truth, it is unlikely that the related elaborate foundation myth centred around the exploits of the twin brothers Romulus and Remus contains many grains of historical truth. Nevertheless, this myth was highly potent and hugely important to the self-image of the city of Rome and its inhabitants even into the third and fourth centuries AD and indeed continues to be important today. Did not the fourth-century AD emperor Maxentius name his son Romulus in honour of the city's original founder in the hope that some of the mythic destiny of his forebear would attach itself to him? Ironically, was not the last Roman ruler of the Western empire the hapless Romulus Augustulus?

ROMULUS AND REMUS AND OTHER FOUNDATION MYTHS

The story of Romulus and Remus begins in the city of Alba Longa in the Alban Hills in the central Italian district of Latium, about 12 miles to the south-east of the site of Rome. The city was ruled by King Numitor, who had two sons and a daughter called Rhea Silvia. Numitor had an ambitious and duplicitous younger brother, called Amulius, who sought to plot against him and indeed eventually deposed him, slaying his sons, whom he saw as a potential threat. Rhea Silvia was allowed to live but was forced by her uncle to become a Vestal Virgin, thus to renounce her sexuality and dedicate her life to the service of the goddess Vesta as a virgin. It was intended through this that she would remain forever barren and produce no heirs to threaten Amulius's power. But this attempt to wipe out Numitor's line was inevitably thwarted by the actions of the gods, and Mars sought out Rhea Silvia and sired two sons with her, the twin boys Romulus and Remus. As a result, Amulius imprisoned Rhea Silvia and the twin babies were placed in a basket which was then thrown into the River Tiber, in flood at the time, with the intention that they would drown. However, fortuitously the basket floated to safety and the twins were found on the banks by a she-wolf who suckled and nurtured them and a woodpecker who brought them food. Both the wolf and the woodpecker were creatures sacred to Mars. Eventually the infants were discovered by the shepherd Faustulus, who took them home and with his wife Acca Larentia raised them to maturity.

As youths, the brothers were headstrong and courageous but slightly out of control. Remus was arrested and brought before the exiled former king Numitor, whose path he had crossed. Romulus rescued Remus and revealed to Numitor that they were his grandsons. Together the three led an army to Alba Longa and deposed the usurper Amulius, restoring Numitor to his rightful throne.

Subsequently the twins went off to found a city of their own on the site of Rome, a schism between the two brothers allegedly being brought about by disagreements over the precise siting of the settlement. Recourse to the ritual of augury to establish the will of the gods by examining the flight of birds in the area apparently favoured Romulus. He therefore founded his own fortified enclosure on the Palatine Hill while Remus set up another enclosure in competition, possibly on the Aventine Hill. Remus was killed soon after this either by Romulus or by one of his underlings, possibly while trying to breach the defences of the Palatine enclosure. Romulus now became sole founder and ruler of the new city of Rome, named after him.

That the foundation myth involving Romulus still remained potent down the years is well illustrated by the accounts detailing the repair and renovation of the 'casa Romuli', that is Romulus's original hut or a facsimile of it, on the Palatine Hill on a number of occasions following its damage by fire towards the end of the first century BC. Remarkably, it is also possible that this heritage structure was still extant in some form during the reign of Constantine in the fourth century AD.

Again, what for many years was considered to be one of the most famous and iconic Roman works of art referred to by ancient writers – the so-called Capitoline Wolf, which holds pride of place in the Capitoline Museum in Rome – keeps the myth fresh in the minds of museum visitors today. This large, magnificent cast bronze is of a she-wolf suckling the infants Romulus and Remus. Yet this work is not necessarily all that it seems, and some visitors to the museum may not take on board the fact that the work is captioned as either being a pre-Roman Etruscan bronze statue of a wolf with the figures of Romulus and Remus added in the Renaissance period or a medieval bronze wolf with Renaissance additions. Scholarly opinion on the dating of this wonderful statue could not be more divided.

Like all such myths, the basic story of Romulus and Remus apparently became embellished with extra detail down the years. For instance, in his book the *Aeneid,* the Augustan Roman poet Virgil made King Numitor of Alba Longa a descendant of Aeneas, the Trojan prince who had fled from burning Troy. In this way he gave succour to the emperor Augustus's own attempts to link himself with the Trojan hero in his political and artistic propaganda.

Another element of the Roman foundation myth which requires examination here concerns the peopling of the city. For every virgin settlement to survive and thrive it requires a population more or less equal in numbers of men and women, to guarantee the creation of future citizens and a level of birthrate necessary for the continuation of the project. Rome in its early days was possibly destined to fail, given that its population was dominated by young men in Romulus's original armed band or subsequently drawn to the city to serve under him. Rome needed women, and Romulus hatched a plan to procure women for the city by subterfuge and by force of arms, tricking Rome's Sabine neighbours, specifically the men of the tribe, into attending a festival in Rome while sending forces to seize their daughters and bring them forcibly into Rome, where they were pressurised and persuaded to stay as consorts of the Roman men. The Rape of the Sabine Women, as this event is known, whether truth or myth, casts a dark shadow over the early history of Rome when viewed from a twenty-first-century Western perspective that frowns upon the equation of war with sexual conquest and rape.

A City on Seven Hills

From a geographical point of view, the site of Rome had a number of natural advantages. Most importantly, it was the first possible crossing point of the River Tiber from the sea and was therefore ideally suited for settlement. It was only about 12 miles inland, with the river's navigability for almost another 50 miles further upstream providing the nascent city with a readily reached hinterland of fertile plains with rich volcanic soils. Secondly, there could be found here seven major hills, more properly actually ridges, subsequently named by the Romans as the Quirinal Hill, the Esquiline Hill, the Caelian Hill, the Aventine Hill, the Capitoline Hill, the Palatine Hill and the Velian Hill, along with a number of minor ones too. Settlement could take place on these hilltops and settlers were protected against both flooding and other people thanks to the height of the features and their potential for defensive building and from the ready availability of fresh, clear water issuing from springs on the lower slopes of the hills. The disadvantages – particularly that of the low-lying land off the hills was prone to winter flooding and was marshy, foetid and malarial in summer – must have been evident too but must have been deemed to be far outweighed by the natural advantages.

Archaeological excavations have demonstrated beyond doubt that the first

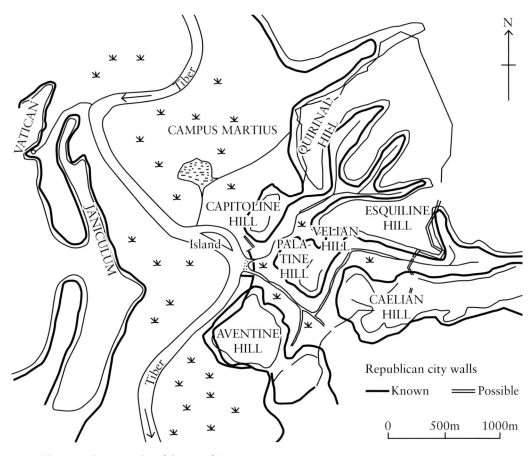

The natural topography of the site of Rome.

major building in Rome took place on the Palatine Hill, although if excavations were conducted to examine the earliest stratigraphic levels on some of the other hills, particularly the Capitoline and Aventine, it is likely that they would show settlement here following on soon after. These separate Iron Age enclosures grew to form small villages which eventually merged into a single large settlement that later became a city.

Given the importance of the Tiber to Rome, it is perhaps surprising that the city did not develop along its axis. Rather, its initial growth was on the eastern side of the river. Crossing the river was nevertheless of paramount importance, and although this might initially have been done by bank-to-bank ferries, the building of permanent bridges must have begun quite early in the life of the settlement. Eight to ten bridges are known from public records and inscriptions, the earliest being the wooden *pons Sublicius*, which dated from the era of the kings, and the latest being the *pons Theodosii* of the late fourth century, connecting the Aventine to Trastevere, though this might simply have been a repaired or rebuilt and rededicated earlier bridge.

The city was only provided with a unified defensive wall system in the late fourth century BC when what is known as the Servian Wall was constructed,

The Pons Fabricius (Ponte Fabricio), the earliest surviving bridge in Rome.

enclosing the seven hills within its 7-mile-long circuit. However, the city continued to expand and spread outside the defences for the next five or six centuries, with little concern for the safety of the undefended areas. But between AD 271 and 275 the emperors Aurelian and Probus set about constructing a new, longer defensive circuit of walls – the 12-mile-long Aurelian Walls – that took in not only the seven hills but also the *Campus Martius* and the area of Trastevere on the west bank of the Tiber. The building of the Aurelian walls, in response to barbarian incursions across the empire, represented the moment when the rulers and people of the city of Rome suddenly lost confidence in their historic invincibility.

While the early settlement was well served by springs and by the digging of wells, as the settlement grew into a city and its needs for ready supplies of fresh water increased exponentially the necessity to provide water presented a direct challenge to Roman engineers. In considering this problem they came up with ingenious solutions which involved the provision of aqueducts and the building of a massive sewerage system in order to address both the shorter-term needs of the inhabitants and the longer-term requirements regarding the city's public health.

The water from the Tiber was polluted, so clean water had to be channelled into the city from outside; the first aqueduct, the *Aqua Appia*, was built in 312 BC and brought water to a public fountain in the cattlemarket – the *Forum Boarium* – from a river source over 10 miles away. By the third century AD Rome had eleven aqueducts supplying private homes, latrines, public baths, fountains and the city's numerous gardens. For most of their length the water ran underground, in lined conduits, but in certain places the aqueduct had to be carried on bridgework, much of which survives today, still standing in and around the city as spectacular reminders of ancient engineering and problem-solving. Even more astonishing surviving examples can be found in some of the Roman provinces. Regular repair and maintenance of the system would have been onerous but necessary.

The area of what was to become the Forum was originally a marsh prone to flooding from the Tiber and probably a malarial swamp in summer. The same applied to the *Campus Martius*, which for much of the Republican era remained marshy open space used for military training. Although a small number of temples were built here, it was not until the time of Augustus that the area was developed and graced with significant architectural commissions, including both the Augustan Altar of Peace – the *Ara Pacis* – and Augustus's mausoleum. Julius Caesar's earlier grand scheme to divert the Tiber and drain the remaining marshes never came to fruition.

The Roman aqueduct at Pont du Gard, near Nîmes, France.

In order to drain such areas of marshy, low-lying land in the city and to dispose of human waste products, the *Cloaca Maxima,* or 'Greatest Sewer', was dug around 600 BC, running through the Forum and discharging into the Tiber. The original outlet can still be seen today near the Ponte Rotto. Initially probably no more than a large open drain flushed by water from diverted streams, this was later fully lined and built over. Subsidiary branch sewers and drains feeding into the *Cloaca Maxima* were built on a piecemeal basis as the city grew. With the provision of the aqueducts huge quantities of used water from the baths and other buildings could then be used to flush through the sewers.

Another natural feature that became integrated into the layout of the city was an island in the Tiber, towards the southern bend in the river. Known to the Romans as the *Insula Tiberina*, this narrow, quarter-mile-long island soon became connected to the city on both banks by two bridges. Almost inevitably, given the propensity for self-mythologising among the Roman people, a legendary origin for the island was promulgated that saw it coming into being when the dead body of the last king of Rome and tyrant Tarquinius Superbus was thrown into the Tiber in 510 BC and mud and silt collected around his corpse to create a mini-island that grew in size as more material collected there. Another version of the story has the irate people of Rome raiding the former tyrant's grain stores and throwing the grain into the river at this point, where again it formed an obstacle around which silt collected and an island formed.

In 293 BC, Roman historians tell us that the city was struck by a great plague. It was at this time that a decision was made to use the *Insula Tiberina* for isolating the sick, and a temple to the healing god Aesculapius was founded there. Other shrines to healing deities followed and the island became associated with this healing role even into the post-Roman medieval period. Possibly in homage to the ship that brought the cult statue of Aesculapius to the island, the Roman authorities built walls around the perimeter of the island, narrowing towards one end in the form of a ship's prow to create the illusion of the island being a ship on the river.

Ports and Docks

South of the Tiber island, where the river took a ninety-degree bend to create a small plain lying at the foot of the Capitoline, Palatine and Aventine hills, the first port of Rome – *Portus Tiberinus* – was established, with a natural landing for smaller boats coming upriver from the sea. The *Forum Boarium,* or cattle market, and the *Forum Holitorium,* or vegetable market, would grow up here to sell goods and beasts fresh off the boats, at a major road junction that further enhanced the suitability of the site. In the late third or early second century BC larger port facilities were built on the wide plain to the south-west of the Aventine Hill, with substantial wharves and a huge warehouse known as the *Porticus Aemilia*, which was later rebuilt in concrete, today a partially standing monument representing the oldest example of a concrete structure in the city.

No discussion of the development of Rome and its empire would be complete without mention of Ostia and Portus, the ports of Rome that handled its huge maritime import and export trade and the seaborne movement of troops when necessary. Ostia, at the Tiber's mouth 20 miles away, was founded in 386 BC and grew rapidly as the horizons of the Roman world expanded, turning into both a port and a small city, as visitors to the startlingly well-preserved remains can see today.

However, Ostia as a river port could not keep pace with the eventual volume of trade, nor with the large seagoing vessels that could not dock there. Indeed, for two hundred years such vessels had to dock in the natural maritime harbour at Puteoli, over 100 miles south on the Bay of Naples, which was the principal maritime facility for Republican Rome.

Portus, 20 miles south-west of the city and a couple of miles north of Ostia, was an artificial deep-water harbour at the Tiber's mouth established by the emperor Claudius in AD 46 and built from scratch to supplement and eventually supersede both Ostia and Puteoli and which was later substantially enlarged and provided with enhanced facilities under Trajan, including a second harbour basin and more warehousing for the storage of goods in transit. The port also had a dry dock and shipyard and a lighthouse stood nearby to guide ships in and out of the harbour. A vast office complex probably housed the administrative and bureaucratic service required for running the port and, most importantly, for registering ships and cargoes and levying taxes. It has been suggested that up to five hundred large ships could now be docked here at any one time and that the port's labour force could have been between 10,000 and 15,000 people. The harbour now lies 2 miles inland, some of it under Rome's Fiumicino airport, due to coastal changes.

Ostia.

Thus Rome's natural situation encouraged the foundation of a city here and allowed for its development as a vital trading centre whose thirst for finding and creating new markets eventually helped fuel its drive towards empire building. One of the most curious sites to visit when in Rome is the large hill known as Monte Testaccio, literally 'the mountain of ceramic', behind the river port facilities that included the *Porticus Aemilia*. This 'hill' is around 115 feet high and covers an area of around 220,000 square feet at its base. It is not a natural feature; rather it is a huge, structured rubbish dump made up of an estimated 53 million broken pottery amphorae or storage vessels for imported olive oil, vessels which could not be cleaned and reused, testifying to the massive volume of trade, which in turn inevitably impacted on the very fabric of the city in this unusual way.

Ostia.

2

FROM REPUBLIC TO EMPIRE: THE HISTORY OF THE CITY OF ROME AND OF THE ROMAN WORLD

The transformation of a series of Tiber valley villages or hamlets into a single unified proto-urban settlement and thence eventually into a city state was achieved over several hundred years. That the unified settlement was first ruled by a succession of Etruscan kings is beyond dispute. The overthrow of these kings and the replacement of royal rule by a republican system that can at last be described as distinctively and truly Roman, marked a tumultuous transformation which in itself gave the city the power structures which would allow it to raise its own citizen armies and eventually to expand its immediate territory through force of arms and sheer political will.

The almost imperceptible Roman conquest of its immediate neighbours, area by area and people by people, eventually snowballed to encompass the conquest of the whole of Italy. A thirst for expansionism was driven by the motor of the commercial wealth that accompanied it in the form of plundered booty, slaves, and taxes levied on newly conquered cities and territories. As the young men of these territories could also now be forcibly conscripted to fight for Rome, the drive towards the creation of an empire beyond the borders of Italy became all-encompassing.

It was indeed the Roman army, its organisation, recruitment strategies, training methods, equipment, tactics, welfare systems and leadership that allowed for this cycle of expansion to take place. A property qualification for enlistment made the earliest Roman citizen force an elitist organisation, the eventual revocation of the property qualification leading to the creation of a more representative and professional army. The mature Roman army was not some kind of invincible 'war machine', as certain military historians have dubbed it; rather, it was simply more efficient more often than most of the opponents it encountered. A legion was made up of 5,000 infantrymen, all Roman citizens, the size of the legionary forces reaching its peak in the second century AD when around 150,000 men served under their banners. The non-citizen auxiliary troops, both cavalry and infantry and in some cases organised into more specialised units, were in many cases recruited en masse from conquered territories. Retired legionaries were given grants of land or a financial pay-off, while retired auxiliary soldiers received Roman citizenship. It is worth noting, though, that the first- and second-century AD army, made up of legions and auxiliaries based in fortresses and forts, was very different indeed from the smaller, mobile field armies of the fourth century, bolstered by the growing recruitment of barbarian troops.

FROM THE KINGS TO THE REPUBLIC

The names of the supposed seven kings of Rome, starting with Romulus, were Numa Pompilius, Tullus Hostilius, Ancus Marcius, Lucius Tarquinius Priscus, Servius Tullius and Lucius Tarquinius Superbus, the last king, who was finally overthrown in 509 BC. Unusually the king was chosen by election of the people and it may have been the case that the last three kings, who were related and were known collectively as the Tarquins, were resented for their attempts to usurp the system and establish some form of dynastic rule. However, it was a much more shocking incident that is reported to have precipitated the crisis leading to the Tarquins' downfall. According to various accounts by Roman historians, the already feared and mistrusted Lucius Tarquinius Superbus was away from Rome campaigning when his son Sextus Tarquinius was accused of raping Lucretia, a member of an established Roman aristocratic family. Lucretia killed herself after making the accusation, and her cause was then taken up by a group of rightly aggrieved citizens led by Lucius Junius Brutus, who first guaranteed the support of the people, then the political elite and then the army. Faced with demands for justice for Lucretia and broader demands for the establishment of a republic, and denied entry into Rome, the king went into exile with his family, never to return, though a number of serious attempts were made by him to do so.

The Roman Republic thus came into being around 510–509 BC, with royal rule replaced by a system which placed power in the hands of two annually elected consuls, the first of whom were Brutus and Lucius Tarquinius Collatinus, and other, lesser magistrates. An advisory council known as the Senate was at first appointed by the consuls. Ironically these first two consuls of Rome were both blood relatives of Lucius Tarquinius Priscus, Rome's fifth king, and suspicion of their motives in seeking power would eventually lead to Collatinus being forced from office and into exile himself. Brutus, meanwhile, won the trust of the people by overseeing the execution of his own sons for plotting the royal return. Brutus died in battle against Tarquin forces and received a magnificent state funeral.

Control of the Roman republican system soon became the almost exclusive preserve of a few powerful aristocratic families and discord in the city over this was inevitable. As inequality between the classes in Rome grew exponentially, so did the displeasure of the city's poorer majority, the plebs, from the late fifth century BC onwards. In the fourth century the brothers Tiberius and Gaius Gracchus, commonly known simply as the Gracchi, became the champions of the plebeian party, standing up for those in the lowest strata of Roman citizenry, eventually leading to their deaths, the first by assassination and the second by suicide under intense hatred and pressure. The great significance of the careers of these two brothers was underlined by the fact that the basal plinth of a statue voted to their mother after her death in 100 BC, aged either ninety or ninety-one, bore an inscription which translates as 'Cornelia, mother of the Gracchi'. This is one of only a handful of statues to women erected in republican Rome and was therefore highly significant.

Between the fifth and third centuries BC, Roman armies conquered all of peninsular Italy and annexed numerous territories, including those of the once powerful Etruscans. Attention would now be turned overseas. However, it was not always forward momentum and Rome's expansionist project suffered a severe setback and test of its mettle in 390 BC when a force of Gauls under their leader Brennus defeated the Roman army at the Battle of the Allia and, three years later, sacked Rome and indeed occupied part of the city for several months, laying siege to the defended Capitoline Hill, where allegedly and famously the cries of penned geese alerted the defenders to the Gauls, who were eventually expelled by the return of the exiled Marcus Furius Camillus. It would be many years before the Romans were able to finally curb the expansionist tendencies of the Gauls.

The wars against Carthage – the Punic Wars – and its great general Hannibal represented one of the most severe tests of the Roman Republic. The inevitable initial clash between these two emerging empires came about in 264 BC when the Romans invaded and annexed Sicily, thus threatening Carthage's well-established trade routes across the Mediterranean. Over a century of conflict followed, including wars in Macedonia, ending in 146 BC with the razing of the city of Carthage itself, but not before Hannibal and his army had crossed the Alps, invaded Italy and inflicted one of the greatest defeats the Roman army would ever suffer at the Battle of Cannae, where around 70,000 Romans were killed. Following the eventual defeat of Carthage, Rome created its own province of Africa and had a foothold on the Iberian Peninsula, which it would soon extend. By 100 BC Greece and much of the Aegean, parts of Asia Minor and further parts of north Africa had been conquered. The Mediterranean Sea, which the Romans now dominated, was their lifeline, allowing them to trade extensively overseas and to maintain their empire, so much so that it became known to them simply as *Mare Nostrum* – Our Sea.

However, the centre could not hold and the Roman world was now inevitably riven by almost a century of internecine power struggles between rival generals; first between Marius and Sulla in 88–82 BC, following their previous alliance and victory in the so-called Social Wars of 90–88 BC; next between Pompey the Great, Crassus and Julius Caesar between 49 and 45 BC; and finally between Octavian (later to be renamed Augustus) and Mark Antony between 44 and 31 BC.

Probable portrait of Julius Caesar.
(© Trustees of the British Museum)

Julius Caesar, or Gaius Julius Caesar to give him his full name, was born into a patrician Roman family in 100 BC. Thrown into danger by his political and family connections to Marius, as a teenager he wisely left Rome to take up a career in the Roman army and served with apparent distinction until he felt it was safe to return to Rome in 78 BC, on the death of the dictator Sulla, from which point on he became a notable legal advocate. Famously he was kidnapped by pirates while crossing the Aegean by ship and on gaining freedom hunted down his captors and, as he had promised them, had them all crucified, possibly as much for their request for a lesser ransom than Caesar believed he was worth, as for their aggression towards him.

The stage was set for this swashbuckling ex-military man to enter politics, and he was duly elected tribune, quaestor, Pontifex Maximus (chief priest of the state religion), praetor and finally consul, the highest magistracy of the Republic, in 59 BC. He also served as a provincial governor and it was during the holding of one such post that he was able to fulfil his military and political ambitions with the invasion and conquest of Gaul in 58–49 BC. We are lucky to have Caesar's own account of the wars in his book *De Bello Gallico – The Gallic Wars* – and though Caesar can at times be a highly unreliable narrator, and passes off material known to have been gathered by other writers as his own, this book is hugely informative on the appearance, behaviour, customs and beliefs of the Gallic and British tribes, providing us with the first detailed accounts of these ahistorical Iron Age peoples. Caesar crossed the channel to Britain twice, in 55 and 54 BC, and though his own account of these expeditions, rather than invasions as such, painted them as hugely successful – hostages being taken, tribute being received and friendship to Rome being pledged by certain of the British tribes – it would appear that such minor successes were only short-term gains.

Between 49 and 45 BC, Julius Caesar, Pompey the Great and Marcus Licinius Crassus formed what was known as the First Triumvirate, but they soon cast their alliance asunder to grapple for personal power in a series of bloody civil wars from which Caesar finally emerged victorious and assumed the reigns of power in Rome, being declared dictator by the Senate. This move was viewed as little short of calamitous to the very existence and safety of the Roman Republic by a group of senators led by Marcus Julius Brutus, and a conspiracy to do away with Caesar was then hatched. The assassination of Julius Caesar on 15 March 44 BC near the theatre of Pompey in Rome is probably the most famous single event in Roman history, and set in motion a power struggle for succession that would cripple the functioning of the Roman state for decades to come. Rather than saving the Republic, the assassins precipitated its end.

The Ara Pacis, Rome.

The subsequent civil war and struggle for succession principally involved Octavian (later to be renamed Augustus), who, as Caesar's heir, was hypothetically defending the Republic on behalf of the Senate, and Mark Antony, Caesar's right-hand man. The war ranged widely across the Mediterranean between 44 and 31 BC. A temporary alliance between Octavian, Antony and Marcus Lepidus – the Second Triumvirate – led to the defeat of Brutus and Cassius, the principal plotters against Caesar, but this shaky alliance soon fell apart as well. The conflict reached its endgame with Octavian's victory over a joint Roman and Egyptian fleet under Mark Antony and Cleopatra at the Battle of Actium in 31 BC

IMPERIAL ROME

The victory of Octavian at Actium more or less represented the end of the war of succession. He returned to Rome as consul, with Marcus Agrippa as second consul, and accepted the title of Augustus – 'powerful one' – from the Senate in 27 BC and subsequently accrued more titles, honours and responsibilities, so much so that he remained Rome's unchallenged ruler until his death in AD 14. However, Augustus cleverly, perhaps cynically, began to style himself as *primus*

The Arch of Titus, Rome.

inter pares' – 'the first among equals' – so that while establishing himself as sole ruler of Rome and its empire Augustus also duplicitously presented himself as the guarantor of the lost values of the old Roman Republic.

Augustus's reign ushered in an extended period of peace and prosperity in Rome and saw the creation of the imperial system, setting the bar almost impossibly high for the 138 Roman emperors who were to follow him up to AD 395, as we shall see in the next chapter. Many of these emperors instead left their mark on Rome in the form of major civic monuments, buildings and artworks.

Up to the reign of Trajan (AD 98–117) the Roman Empire was in a state of constant expansion, a process that was brought to a halt by his successor, Hadrian. No new provinces were added to the empire after Dacia's seizure in AD 106. The system of imperial rule was to be sorely tested by wars on both the northern and eastern frontiers from the reign of Marcus Aurelius onwards (AD 161–180). In the third century AD it is generally accepted that the Roman world was in crisis, though the precise nature of this crisis and its causes is less subject to a consensus interpretation. Certainly military and political instability was the root cause of the situation, encouraging usurpers and problems at the frontiers and leading to virtual civil war at times, but provincial unease, economic depression and public health emergencies also contributed to the sense of a world

Above: Trajan's Markets, Rome.

Below: The Arch of Constantine, Rome.

spinning out of control. The repeated devaluation and debasement of gold and silver coinage over this period led to a kind of hyperinflation and to spiralling prices for raw materials, basic foodstuffs and other goods, and severe disruption to trade across the empire.

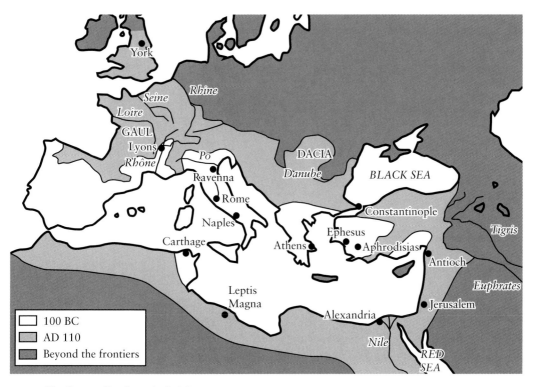

The Roman Empire at its height.

The emperor Diocletian came to power in AD 284, and during his twenty-year reign set about addressing the economic and political situation in novel ways that had escaped his flailing predecessors. Certainly Diocletian's root-and-branch reform of the imperial administration and the tax system, his provincial reorganisation and the issuing of the Edict on Maximum Prices represented inspired solutions.

Diocletian rightly and wisely saw that the empire was now too vast and complex an entity for one man to rule alone, even with a strong army, and introduced a new system of imperial authority called the Tetrarchy, literally 'the rule of four'. It was intended that the system's built-in division of responsibilities would militate against the power plays and rivalries between high-ranking generals and emperors that had led to the political anarchy of the previous five decades or so. The empire was to be divided administratively into two parts, the west and the east. A senior and a junior emperor were to serve at the same time in each of the two parts, thus guaranteeing an orderly succession in the case of the death of one of the tetrarchs. The system even allowed for the abdication of a serving senior emperor – a function Diocletian himself exercised in AD 305 – and his immediate replacement by the elevation of a junior emperor to senior rank and the appointment of a new junior.

Revenues generated through the tax system were crucial to the running of the Roman imperial administration, which required vast sums of money on an assured and regular basis to maintain its extensive bureaucracy. Just as the Roman Empire had been created in a piecemeal fashion, so too had the tax system evolved

Statue of the Tetrarchs, St Mark's Square, Venice.

to reflect local practices across the empire, with all the attendant problems that unfair variations and exemptions can create. Diocletian's new tax system of AD 296 introduced a unified system of land and poll taxes for all provinces and, most significantly, for Italy as well.

Diocletian's reorganisation of the provincial system was the most thorough and far-reaching since the time of Augustus, intended not simply to limit the amount of power that could be held or accrued by any one individual but also to increase efficiency and create parity between Italy and the provinces. The reform of the military command structure was crucial to this programme. Despite the fact that the administrative subdivision of many provinces inevitably led to a swollen bureaucracy, the system proved relatively successful and remained Diocletian's key legacy to the empire long after his death.

Diocletian's Edict on Maximum Prices of AD 301 represents the best-documented, longest and most detailed economic plan that has come down to us from the ancient world and provides startling and fascinating insights into the complexity and diversity of Roman trade and the procurement and sale of goods and services both in Rome and across the empire. The edict was not intended

As might have been expected, caps were introduced for the prices of basic foodstuffs by weight, such as cereals of various kinds, beans and pulses and rice, for meats and fish, for oils, for salt, for wines and beers. For instance, no one was to pay more than ten *denarii* for a pound of beef mincemeat or sixteen *denarii* for ten brace of sparrows. No one was to pay more than one hundred *denarii* for a pound of washed wool from Asturia in Spain or twelve thousand *denarii* for a pound of white silk, presumably bought through intermediary traders with the Far East. If you wished to employ a scribe to write one hundred lines of text in the best hand then the edict set the price for this service at twenty-five *denarii*. A teacher of arithmetic was to be paid seventy-five *denarii* per boy taught per month. A carpenter could charge no more than fifty *denarii* a day, a sewer cleaner twenty-five *denarii*, and a camel driver twenty-five *denarii*. From a British perspective it is interesting to note that a hooded British wool cloak referred to in the edict as the *birrus Britannicus* could be sold for no more than six thousand *denarii*.

simply as a toothless guidance document but was backed up by clear sanctions involving execution or exile for anyone who charged or paid higher prices than those stated in the edict and for speculative hoarders and what we might call black marketeers.

If Diocletian's sweeping political, military, administrative and financial reforms represented a daring move to address some of the most pressing issues of his day, ultimately they can be said to have failed. Perhaps the administrative reorganisation of the provinces was most crucial in temporarily stabilising the empire. The Tetrarchy fell apart as the tetrarchs jostled among themselves for supremacy and reverted to arms and civil war to resolve their differences. Eventually Constantine would be the last tetrarch standing and would return the empire to his sole rule and to the rule of his dynasty. The Maximum Price Edict was eventually revoked. If perhaps too rosy a picture of Diocletian as emperor has been painted here, then it should be remembered that his reign was also marked by the systematic and increased state persecution of Christians, almost as scapegoats. The emperor also singularly failed to address the most pressing problem of the era: the incursions of barbarian peoples over the frontiers. Military reorganisation alone could not tackle this almost intractable problem, which helped lead to the end of the Western Roman Empire, as we will see in a later chapter.

Thus our brief historical overview has taken us from the founding of a number of Iron Age villages in an open, natural landscape, to the same group of settlements merging and growing to become the vast, vibrant metropolis that was ancient Rome. Its sophisticated political system, professional army and driving will to power allowed it first to dominate Italy and then to establish an empire that encompassed the whole of the Mediterranean and lands beyond. In a period such as the third and fourth centuries AD, marked by political change and crisis, such an empire was not sustainable and despite attempts at swinging reform the Roman Empire entered the fifth century with rightful trepidation.

3

THE EMPERORS OF ROME: AUGUSTUS TO CONSTANTINE

It should be no surprise to learn that of Rome's emperors between Augustus in the first century BC and Constantine in the fourth century AD, among them were both good and bad emperors, along with very many indifferent wearers of the imperial purple, most of these indifferent emperors rising almost without trace to reign briefly in the troubled third century AD.

AUGUSTUS

Augustus (reigned 31 BC–AD 14) was the first emperor and came to power following the bitter civil war set off by Julius Caesar's murder. Augustus's reported boast that he found Rome a city of brick and left it a city of marble very much reflects the extraordinary surge in public building projects in the city during his long reign, which established a trend for imperial architectural patronage as a symbol of benign authority. He also reorganised the administrative areas of the city into fourteen regions, as opposed to the previous four, sub-divided into neighbourhood units.

Augustus left to us an important document known as the *Res Gestae*, a form of checklist of his achievements which was to be inscribed on bronze tablets set up in front of his mausoleum in Rome for all to see. The versions we have today were copies set up elsewhere in the empire in order to spread word of his death and deification. The text of the document addresses the Roman people and is as interesting for what it omits to tell us as it is for its content. It is in this document that the emperor lists the major building projects he commissioned and personally financed in Rome, which helped turn the city of brick into a city of marble. After briefly describing his entry into public life, he details his military victories, before listing all the honours bestowed on him by the Roman people as well as the senate. He then exhaustively lists his expenditures and successes in foreign wars. There is little in the document on his moral legislation aimed at regulating the proper behaviour of the women of Rome, which had such a profound impact on Roman society at the time.

Opposite: Augustus and the imperial family on the Gemma Augustea. (Courtesy of R. Gifford)

Below left: The so-called Prima Porta statue of Augustus. (Vatican Museums, Rome)

Below right: Augustus as chief priest. (National Roman Museum, Rome)

We must also remember that although they did not formally control any part of the running of the state, the Roman empresses nevertheless held a considerable amount of personal power, none more so than Livia, wife of Augustus and the first empress of Rome. The potent power of images in the age of Augustus could not be better summed up than in the reliefs on the Augustan Altar of Peace in Rome, known as the *Ara Pacis Augustae*, on which both Augustus and Livia appear and where images of family, family solidarity, fertility, abundance and peace jostle for the viewer's attention, the overall message conveyed being that Augustus has brought peace and stability to the whole Roman world, ironically through war. Just as Augustus carefully created and manipulated his image through artistic propaganda in the form of portrait statues and his bust on coins, so too did Livia. Outliving her husband by some years, she subtly changed her persona to that of mother of the new emperor Tiberius, and by doing so retained much of her power and the affection of the Roman people. Just as Augustus had been deified – officially made into a god – by order of the Roman senate, so too was Livia granted this honour on her death in AD 29.

Left: The empress Livia. (National Roman Museum, Rome)

Below: The empress Livia on the Ara Pacis, Rome.

THE GOOD EMPERORS

The so-called 'good emperors' of the Roman Empire's first few centuries were universally acknowledged to be Nerva, Trajan, Hadrian, Antoninus Pius and Marcus Aurelius, also collectively known as the adoptive emperors. Their combined eighty-four-year reign would be looked back upon with nostalgia as representing some kind of golden age for both the city of Rome and the Roman Empire in general.

Nerva (reigned AD 96–98) is perhaps the least well known of the five. He was already sixty-six years old at the time of his selection as emperor by the Roman Senate, and childless. Although his reign was very short, his even-handedness and political acuity, gained through years of experience as a senator himself, brought stability to the city after the almost random excesses of his autocratic predecessor Domitian, whose virulent unpopularity was reflected in his eventual assassination. Not only did Nerva institute a return to the rule of law, but he was also responsible for guaranteeing a painless succession by his wise and inspired choice of Trajan as his adopted son. Nerva also set in train an alimentary programme for feeding the poor that Trajan was to continue and expand.

Trajan (reigned AD 98–117) was the first of the soldier-emperors and the first emperor since Augustus to make a major impact on the very appearance of the city of Rome itself. Not only did he undertake risky and adventurous wars against the Dacians, favouring further expansion of the empire, he also reinvested the colossal amounts of booty from those wars of conquest in vast new building projects in the centre of Rome, including a huge new Forum, bigger in size than all the earlier Forums put together, a major new baths complex and an enormous market complex which very explicitly made real the connection between conquest and commerce, as did a new harbour at Rome's port of Ostia. Trajan's cremated remains were buried in the base of the decorated column built in his honour by his successor that today bears his name and whose novel helical frieze illustrates episodes from the emperor's Dacian Wars.

Hadrian (reigned AD 117–138), although adopted by Trajan in the same way that he had been officially adopted as successor by Nerva, could not have been more different from his predecessor in character and in actions. Bearded in the fashion of a Greek philosopher, Hadrian was a thoughtful, ruminative ruler and an intellectual one. He spent a considerable period of his reign travelling around the provinces of the empire – he visited Britain in AD 122 for instance – and observing the workings of the imperial system at first hand. The lessons learned appear to have informed his adopted policy of retrenchment and consolidation. He made a lesser mark on Rome's skyline than had Trajan but nevertheless left a considerable architectural legacy in the city, and he should be remembered in particular for his commissioning of the building of the Pantheon, a temple to all the gods, a magnificent, hemispherically domed structure that still stands intact today, as well as remarkable frontier works in a number of provinces, most notably Britain, where impressive portions of Hadrian's Wall still survive as a major heritage site.

If a frisson of excitement among the Roman public had been generated by gossip about Nerva's doddery infirmity, about Trajan's childlessness and implied infertility and about Hadrian's reported infatuation with the Bithynian male youth Antinuous, then the reign of Antoninus Pius (reigned AD 138–161) must have silenced the gossips for nigh on two decades, so comparatively dull and uneventful was it. The emperor seldom travelled outside of Italy and led a seemingly blameless life, happily married, conservative in his policies and careful with imperial wealth, little of which went on the kind of prestigious building projects in Rome which his immediate predecessors had favoured. He also again demonstrated great wisdom in making Marcus Aurelius his adopted son and heir.

Hadrian. (Thassos Museum, Greece)

Marcus Aurelius (reigned AD 161–180) spent the greater part of his reign away from Rome, campaigning on the northern and eastern frontiers where barbarian incursions were becoming highly problematic and dangerous to the overall security of the empire. The emperor is best known to us today for his philosophical, but highly personal, book *Meditations*, which balances a stoical perspective on life with a mystical dimension that firmly places man within a cosmic whole and at one with nature. An emphasis on moral probity foregrounds the contribution to life overall of 'the good man', much as Marcus himself appears to have been. His impact on Rome from an architectural point of view was relatively minimal, although he did oversee the commemoration of Antoninus Pius and Faustina by the erection of a memorial column to them in the *Campus Martius*.

It was over a hundred years until another emperor generally judged by his contemporaries and by later historians to be 'good' reigned. Constantine (reigned AD 306–337), also known as Constantine the Great or Constantine I, is often viewed as the last really great emperor of Rome, a man who oversaw the transformation of Rome from a pagan to a Christian city – a somewhat oversimplified interpretation of his actions and motives. In the later part of his reign Constantine was to make a decision that had a fundamental impact on the city of Rome and in many ways diminished its power and prestige, a decision which forever after would be seen as greatly to the city's detriment. This was the founding in AD 330 of Constantinople, a 'new Rome' at the ancient city of Byzantium on the Bosporus in Turkey. It would appear to have left the Senate of Rome feeling betrayed and outmanoeuvred by the emperor, who transferred his court there, though Rome still maintained its status as the mother city of the empire.

An equestrian statue of Marcus Aurelius, Campidoglio, Rome.

Left: Head of colossal statue of Constantine. (Capitoline Museums, Rome)

Below: Hand of colossal statue of Constantine. (Capitoline Museums, Rome)

At the head of a shortlist of emperors on whom history has not yet made a definitive judgement, good or bad, is Maxentius (reigned AD 306–312), who died at the hands of Constantine's army just outside of the city of Rome at the Battle of the Milvian Bridge in AD 312, drowning in the churning waters of the River Tiber. While he is described as a tyrant in the inscription on the Arch of Constantine built in honour of the victorious emperor by the senate, it would appear that Maxentius was one of the few emperors of the late third and early fourth centuries AD to pay much attention to the city of Rome itself, and by basing himself there and commissioning many new building projects he won the approval of both the senate and the people of Rome. Indeed, no emperor since Septimius Severus (reigned AD 193–211) had done as much, and Severus had to some extent been forced to sponsor extensive rebuilding in the aftermath of another major fire in the city in AD 192. Many of the great buildings in Rome dedicated by Constantine were in fact originally conceived under Maxentius, and indeed Constantine's imprimatur on these schemes simply involved their rededication.

BAD EMPERORS

Because Augustus had set such a remarkable precedent in good governance during his long reign, it was almost inevitable that his immediate successors would be harshly judged in comparison. Indeed, this was to be the case. In AD 121 the historian Suetonius published his famous book, known to us today as *The Twelve Caesars*, providing gossipy and often scabrous and devastatingly critical portraits of Julius Caesar and Rome's first eleven emperors – Augustus, Tiberius, Caligula, Claudius, Nero, Galba, Otho, Vitellius, Vespasian, Titus and Domitian. In this history we learn of Julius Caesar's obvious comb-over to hide his baldness and his vain weeping before a statue of Alexander the Great because Alexander had achieved so much in his short life while Caesar had achieved so little; by Caesar's age Alexander had conquered all the known world, he explained. Suetonius tells us that Caligula married his own sister and had his horse made consul; that Claudius limped, drooled and had a terrible stutter; that Nero played music while Rome burned; and that Vespasian's last words were reported as being 'I think I'm turning into a god', a cynical dig by the author at what he obviously viewed as the ridiculous system of deification and the worship of emperors and selected members of their families through the imperial cult.

Of the outright bad emperors, Nero (reigned AD 54–68) perhaps represented the most hated figure of his time, a judgement shared by many subsequent historians. It was during his reign in AD 64 that one of the most devastating fires Rome would ever see destroyed vast swathes of the city, as the unconcerned emperor was said to be playing his lyre and singing. The emperor subsequently blamed Christians for starting the fire. However, many citizens of the time were reported as being suspicious of the emperor's behaviour and ready to blame him for organising an arson attack to clear an area ready for his own grandiose building scheme, though to be fair this seems highly unlikely.

Commodus (reigned AD 180–192), son of Marcus Aurelius, undoubtedly ranks as one of the worst emperors Rome ever saw. Financially profligate, corrupt in his dealings with opponents, he was both feared and mocked. His increasingly unhinged behaviour, such as his overt identification with the hero god Hercules and his fighting as a gladiator in the arena, provoked a number of assassination attempts and his eventual death by strangulation at the hands of the wrestler Narcissus, who was acting for high-ranking conspirators.

Commodus in the guise of Hercules. (Capitoline Museums, Rome)

In the imperial context it is important to remember that the Romans were very conscious of the concept and workings of historical memory and therefore were equally open in condemning the reign of a particular emperor after his death, as they were in praising him. The most extreme manifestation of this was for the senate to enact a *damnatio memoriae* – literally the damnation of the memory – on a particular imperial person and often too on certain of his relatives, or for emperors to turn the practice on their elite enemies in Rome. The practice had its origins in the republican era and involved the seizing of property of the damned, the erasure of his or her name from publicly displayed inscriptions and the destruction or recarving of their portrait statues; in other words, an attempt to remove them from the historical record and thus from the social memory. For instance, the emperor Domitian was damned in this way, as was Commodus, and Septimius Severus's son Geta was damned at the behest of his brother Caracalla.

IMPERIAL DUTIES

Clothing was highly symbolic in Rome and dress codes were strictly adhered to by all classes. The emperor wore purple clothing to distinguish him above all others, particularly from the senators who customarily wore togas with a wide purple band. The dye for the imperial garments, a product known simply as 'purple', was phenomenally expensive, being distilled from *murex* seashells. On occasions, emperors would wear laurel wreaths or crowns, particularly to celebrate a military victory at a triumph, a form of elaborate military parade. Laurel crowns and triumphs were honours once available to victorious Roman generals under the Republic but in imperial times became honours strictly reserved for the emperor.

At a triumph the emperor would ride at the head of the parade in a chariot, with a slave behind him in the chariot holding a gold crown or laurel wreath over his head. The slave was said to be rehearsed to whisper in the emperor's ear at the giddy height of the ceremony some phrase resembling 'remember you are a mortal', a practice supposedly instituted in order to ground and humble the euphoric emperor at his great moment of success.

From the time of Augustus onwards the duties of the Roman emperor also became synonymous with the carrying out of the rites of the state religion, usually in the role of *Pontifex Maximus*, or chief priest. Thus on so many Roman imperial monuments we see depictions of the emperor of the day, his head usually covered, overseeing the carrying out of a sacrifice, most usually what was known as the *suovetaurilia*, that is the triple sacrifice of a bull, a sheep and a pig.

Above: The Mausoleum of Augustus, Rome.

Below: The Mausoleum of Hadrian, Rome.

DEATH AND THE EMPEROR

Some accounts of great imperial funerals have come down to us, such as those of the emperors Pertinax (died AD 193) and Septimius Severus (died in York in AD 211), while some images of state funerals are also known, such as the reliefs on the pedestal base of the Column of Antoninus Pius dated to AD 161. This evidence allows us to some extent to reconstruct the rites accompanying the celebration of the death of an emperor or other significant imperial family member. A long, grand, formal procession would wind its way down from the Palatine Hill to end up in the Forum, accompanying either the body of the deceased or the deceased in effigy. In the procession would be carried statues or effigies of past great Romans and of personifications of the provinces of the empire. Speeches and eulogies would be delivered from the *rostra,* or speaker's platform, in the Forum to the senate and massive crowds. If the body of the emperor was indeed present, the procession would then depart and move on to the *Campus Martius* for cremation on a vast funeral pyre, accompanied by religious rites and military manoeuvres involving the circling of the pyre. The cremated remains would subsequently be collected for interment in a mausoleum. The funeral would be followed by celebratory games in the arena or by racing at the hippodrome.

The impressive mausolea of several emperors survive to some extent and can be viewed in Rome today, the best of these being the circular Mausoleum of Augustus in the *Campus Martius* and the Mausoleum of Hadrian on the west bank of the Tiber, which was subsequently converted into the Castel Sant'Angelo. The highly impressive mausoleum and sarcophagus of Constantine's mother, the empress Helena, testify to the continuing power and status of the imperial women into the late Roman period.

The Roman system of deifying a dead emperor or empress came into being right at the start of the imperial era, with both Augustus and his wife Livia enjoying this strange honour which gave rise to the empire-wide celebration of a formal imperial cult. The apotheosis or ascent to the heavens of several imperial figures, most notably Augustus, Sabina, the wife of Hadrian, and Antoninus Pius and his wife Faustina, is depicted on imperial monuments, coins and gemstones.

Above: The Mausoleum of the empress Helena, Rome.

Below: The sarcophagus of the empress Helena. (Vatican Museums, Rome)

The apotheosis of Antoninus Pius and Faustina. (Vatican Museums, Rome)

4

THE PEOPLE OF ROME: CITIZENS, FOREIGNERS, SLAVES

The population of Rome once it had become a power outside of Italy was highly cosmopolitan, comprising in the main citizens but with large numbers of foreigners and particularly slaves. At its height in the time of Augustus, the population of the city has been estimated to have been around 1 million people. That it reached this level and maintained this number for centuries afterwards was probably due almost entirely to migration. To put this in some kind of perspective, no city in Europe was to reach such a size again until London did around 1800. Of the million inhabitants, at least a quarter of the population would have comprised slaves.

The spoken and written language of the Romans was, of course, Latin. The majority of the citizens of Rome would probably have been illiterate, but in such a visual society political messages could still be directed at such citizens through the medium of images on coins and commemorative monuments.

CITIZENS

The citizens of Rome comprised two quite distinct social groups by status: the majority ordinary citizens, or plebs, and a small, hierarchical aristocracy including patricians and equestrians which together held most of the power but probably never amounted to more than 2,500 to 3,000 people. Yet the famous Roman acronym *SPQR* (standing for '*Senatus Populusque Romanus*', translated as 'the senate and the people of Rome') quite deliberately stressed the power and indivisibility of the united citizen body of the city.

Freeborn Roman women were classed as citizens but could not vote or hold political office, but could hold a small number of religious offices. Unmarried Roman women derived their status from their fathers and married women from their husbands.

The Roman political system that developed after the expulsion of the last king was complex. The senate was literally a council of elders which in the case of the

Above left: The *Barberini togatus* statue of an aristocratic Roman carrying busts of his ancestors. (Capitoline Museums, Rome)

Above right: A mother and daughter. (Capitoline Museums, Rome)

patriarchal society of Rome meant exclusively male elders. Numbers of senators varied at different times, sometimes one hundred, sometimes two hundred, sometimes three hundred. Initially membership was by appointment only and then by property qualification, allowing certain members of the plebeian class to qualify to become senators. The golden years of the senate were under the Republic; once imperial rule was established the power of the senate was severely diminished, though not necessarily curtailed. Consuls, magistrates and aediles had to be elected annually by the members of the senate. The two consuls under the Republic held an incredible amount of personal power, as we have seen in a previous chapter, but under the Empire consul became little more than an honorary title. Various grades of magistrate such as quaestors, praetors and censors were responsible for well-defined financial or legal roles. The four aediles were responsible for the maintenance of public buildings and the overseeing of arrangements for the numerous public festivals throughout the year in Rome.

Such a system required considerable bureaucratic backup, and there would have been numerous civil servants, as we would call them, running things on a day-to-day basis, including procurators or managers, lawyers, tax collectors, financial controllers, bookkeepers, general clerks and other officials. Out on the streets, crime was monitored by the *vigiles urbani*, set up by Augustus to both protect the city from crime and to fight fires should the need arise. Traditionally the Roman military was not allowed to play any role in the policing of the city, though the elite Praetorian Guard were specifically tasked with protecting the emperor and his family.

Large numbers of people, including slaves, would have been employed as civic workers, maintaining sewers, drains and aqueducts, working on public building projects as stonemasons, carpenters, plumbers or labourers, building and repairing roads, cleaning public buildings, monuments and civic spaces, disposing of rubbish, burying the dead, and so on. The city would have been home to numerous traders and merchants, shopkeepers and others dependant on the city's vibrant import and export trade. A large population such as that of Rome would have needed doctors and midwives, teachers and lawyers. Many more Romans would have worked in what we call the service industries, managing lodging houses for the city's numerous visitors, running inns, making and serving food, working in wholesale and retail, involved in haulage of goods by river or road, manufacturing or crafting goods, carving statues or funerary monuments, striking coins at the city mint, or providing entertainment of one kind or another.

The overwhelming majority of the workers that we have discussed so far would have been men. However, it is known that working women were present in small numbers in Rome and in other Italian towns such as Ostia and Pompeii and in provinces such as Gaul. As well as fulfilling roles such as midwives or nurses we know of female doctors, bar workers, market traders, shop staff, cobblers, textile workers, seamstresses and jewellers.

So it would appear that running in tandem with Rome's slave economy was a kind of free labour market, particularly reliant on the freedmen class of ex-slaves. Diocletian's Edict of Maximum Prices, issued in AD 301, includes references to paid employment in many professions and trades, as we have seen in an earlier chapter.

Right: Funerary relief of a cobbler.
(Capitoline Museums, Rome)

Below: Relief showing working of a mill.
(Vatican Museums, Rome)

A working man unloading a barrel from a docked ship. (National Roman Museum, Rome)

A working woman from Ostia selling poultry. (Ostia Museum)

FOREIGNERS

Foreigners represented a significant proportion of the city's population, maybe as much as 5 per cent at any one time, though some scholars have suggested a far higher percentage, many of them having sought and gained the legal right to undertake commercial transactions in the city. Records indicate that a mechanism existed for the expulsion of foreigners from the city in certain circumstances, indicating that their presence was carefully monitored. The largest individual group was probably ethnic Greek, but it is generally considered that Gauls, Spaniards, people from the European eastern provinces and the Balkans, Egyptians, Syrians, Jews from Palestine and north Africans were also well represented. It is likely that only a handful of Britons ever lived or worked in Rome as free citizens. Indeed, from the north-western provinces we find that only three Britons are recorded by inscriptions, along with 75 Gauls and 137 Germans.

Writing in the first century AD, Seneca noted that many of Rome's people 'have flooded in from the country towns of Italy, in fact from all over the world. And their motives for coming? A hope to get on in the world in some cases, the necessary condition of some public or diplomatic post in others; in others, self-indulgence in search of a good, rich opportunity for vicious living. Some come to Rome for education, others for the games; some to be near their friends, others – workers – because Rome gives them greater scope for displaying their skill. Or they have brought something to sell, a beautiful body or, perhaps, a beautiful voice.'

Almost 1,300 inscriptions recording foreigners at Rome, including military personnel, have been found to date, a figure that is actually likely to be just the tip of the iceberg in overall numerical terms for actual numbers present in the city at any one period. However, this sample does allow us to look at relative numbers of people from different provinces.

It would seem that there were certain areas of the city where its character would have reflected in some way the culture of the people who formed the majority population there, and in Rome at certain times we can identify, for instance, Jewish quarters (the largest of which was probably in what is today's trendy Trastevere district), plus Egyptian and Syrian quarters.

Funerary inscriptions allow us to consider the stories of many named individuals who came to Rome from outside. For instance, trade brought the wine and olive oil merchant Coelia Mascellina to Rome in the second century AD, as we know from the funerary inscription she dedicated there to her parents. Some inscriptions found outside Rome also record foreigners who had spent time in the city, as in the case of a first-century AD funerary inscription set up by a woman called Papiria Rhome from the town of Salona in the Roman province of Dalmatia, in present-day Croatia, recording the fact that her son, Publius Papirius Proculus, aged thirteen, died in Rome, tragically killed by a falling roof tile.

Possible slave collar tag. (© Trustees of the British Museum)

SLAVES

Slavery was crucial not only to the running of the city of Rome itself but also more broadly to the Roman economy, empire building resulting in a greater recourse to the taking of slaves as a boon of conquest. Slaves could also be bought from pirates and brigands, or from slave traders operating among peoples outside of the empire. Slavery also became an ingrained part of Roman urban culture and slaves part of the material culture that defined the city's rich, and particularly its super-rich, citizens. The imperial court would not have been able to function without its own body of slaves, nor would the city's bureaucracy without its public slaves. Bigger and grander private houses needed more and more slaves to run and maintain. Children born of slave parents also automatically became slaves themselves.

If Roman slavery was underpinned by the threat of violence from master or overseer towards their slaves, then it is not altogether surprising to find recurring evidence of slaves turning violently back upon their masters. Everyone is familiar with the large-scale slave revolt in Italy led by the former gladiator or soldier Spartacus in the 70s BC, but many lesser incidents are known, such as the murder

Slaves would be bought and sold at auction, their value dependent on their age, gender, appearance, health, nationality and any special skills or attributes. Male slaves were generally more expensive than female ones; Ethiopian male slaves were highly prized, and dwarfs were apparently quite fashionable in certain circles at certain times. A number of artefacts relating to the life of slaves can bring us up short in surprise and remind us of the crude reality of the system. An inscribed tag on an iron slave collar cajoles the reader to 'restrain me, so that I do not escape, and take me back to my master Pascasius in the colonnade in Trajan's market'. On other tags rewards were offered for the return of the runaway slave wearing the collar. While a fictional character, there must have been many masters like Juvenal's creation Rutilus, who 'to his trembling household … is a complete monster, never happy until he has called for a torturer and some poor wretch is being branded with a hot iron, and all because of two missing towels'.

of Lucius Pedanius Secundus, the prefect of the city of Rome, by one of his four hundred slaves in AD 61.

Yet the Roman system allowed for slaves to be freed – to be granted manumission in a ceremony in which the slave was touched by the *vindicta*, a rod or staff which had probably been used to beat and discipline slaves. This was extremely common and eventually would lead to freedmen becoming a significant and important social class in the city. Gaining manumission was most commonly achieved upon the death of a master and the granting of freedom to his slaves in his will. The sophisticated politician and writer Cicero was a good example of a benign slave owner who treated his slaves humanely. He freed a number of them, most notably his personal secretary, Tiro. Freeing a slave was not necessarily the act of generosity that it might at first appear to be, though; in some cases slaves were freed in this way to flatter the vanity of the owner even in death. Many tombstone epitaphs also testify to quite how common an occurrence it was for a male master to free and then marry one of his female slaves. Slaves could also purchase their freedom from their savings and in a situation such as this the relationship between master and slave now became that of patron and client.

At any one time there would have been 100,000 to 200,000 slaves in the city of Rome, though with the expansion of the empire more or less ending under Hadrian numbers of slaves obtained as war booty obviously tailed off from then onwards.

A freedmen funerary relief from Rome. (National Roman Museum, Rome)

Another freedmen funerary relief from Rome. (National Roman Museum, Rome)

HOUSING

A crucial question to address is, where on earth in Rome did all these people live? The majority poor, middling and reasonably well off would have lived in large, multi-storied apartment blocks, some up to seventy-five feet in height according to Augustan building regulations. These *insulae* would probably in many cases have been occupied by shops and workshops at ground-floor level, with the accommodation above. The occupants of the lower few floors would have enjoyed sanitation and water; those living on the upper floors would have had to make use of communal facilities elsewhere. The richer Romans lived in a *domus*, a private house that varied tremendously in size from something modest to something almost palatial. It has been calculated that there were probably somewhere between 42,000 and 46,000 *insulae* and 1,790 private houses in Rome in the late third century AD, when the city's population was around 750,000.

LIFE EXPECTANCY IN ROME

Historians of ancient demography or population statistics find it difficult to answer what might appear to be a relatively simple question: what was the average life expectancy of the ancient Romans? One might presume, incorrectly as it happens, that it would routinely have been much less than in Western society today. The answer would, of course, have been very much dependent on which class of ancient Romans we are referring to; as in all societies, the poor would have had a lower life expectancy than the rich in many cases. Slaves, of course, were another matter entirely, their life expectancy depended on whether they worked on the docks or in the mines undertaking hard labour, for instance, or whether they were household slaves, clerks or scribes and the like, with perhaps a less arduous and physically demanding routine. We know from inscriptions on funerary monuments that some Romans did live into their nineties and well into the hundreds, so in that society it appears likely that individuals in the right circumstances did indeed have the potential and capacity to reach 115 years of age, the generally accepted maximum age for an individual in the West today. What was different in ancient Rome was the much, much higher risk of death at birth or in early infancy, and the high death rate in the population in general due to infectious diseases, poor sanitation and hygiene, poor medical practices, dietary deficiencies, a greater prevalence of risk and accidents, and warfare.

Life expectancy statistics for ancient Rome might also have been slightly skewed by the poorly understood but attested practice of exposure of unwanted children – predominantly girls, it would appear – and by other methods of infanticide. The practice only formally became culturally and legally unacceptable in the fourth century AD.

CHILDREN

We know relatively little about the lives of Roman children, though we can assume that children of the wealthy had more secure, comfortable and healthy lives than their plebeian counterparts. Again, citizen or freeborn children would have been better off than the children of slaves who themselves were, according to Roman law, technically born into slavery. While there are relatively few extended references to children in Roman writings – though, surprisingly, many nostalgic asides about the freedom of childhood – children are not entirely absent from the archaeological record; their profiles are simply much lower than those of adults for cultural reasons. A Roman child was seen as someone to be prepared, controlled and moulded by their father or to their father's instructions for their allotted place in adult life based upon preordained class roles. Children up to the age of seven lived family lives that precluded any public roles. After seven boys of the elite could expect to start schooling and to become involved in the family's private and public life, including religious and ritual events. Childhood was legally deemed to end for girls at twelve years of age and for boys at fourteen, with betrothal and marriage then on the agenda.

One of the best-known Roman dolls was found in the nineteenth century during the building of the Palazzo di Giustizia in Rome and was inside a sarcophagus containing the body of Crepereia Tryphaena, according to the accompanying inscription, a seventeen-year-old girl who probably died some time in the mid second century AD. Not only was there the exquisite jointed ivory doll with its fashionable contemporary hairstyle, but also a tiny key in the doll's hand to open a small casket of ivory inside the sarcophagus, which contained the doll's own silver mirrors and ivory combs. Crepereia Tryphaena would appear to have died before marriage and therefore the inclusion of the doll as a grave-good can be seen either as a reflection of her unmarried, virginal, almost childlike status or the doll could be seen to represent the fully mature woman that she was yet to grow into. Of course, the doll could simply have been a cherished personal item included here by someone who was familiar with her fondness for the toy.

A Roman doll from the Fayum, Egypt. (© Trustees of the British Museum)

Roman children in their leisure time would have been much like Western children before the internet generation. We know that boys played more outside and ran and swam, skimmed stones on water, built sandcastles when on the coast, pretended to be soldiers, and played with balls, hoops and spinning tops, while girls were more confined indoors and played with similar toys but also with jointed dolls of ivory, bone or wood, most often displaying female adult physical characteristics.

If what we have already learned about Roman childhood implies some degree of indifference to children in general, then we can gain some insight into a more sympathetic and nuanced attitude towards individual children from looking at Roman funerary monuments of various kinds, the commemoration of those who died before reaching adulthood often being touching and pathetic in the true sense of that word. The decorative schemes on Roman children's sarcophagi in particular provide narrative evidence of parental care, devotion and love, and often include scenes of joyously capering and playing children in the guise of cupids or *putti*. Sometimes the child was commemorated in terms of the depiction of the adult life and roles that he or she never lived to assume in the city of Rome.

5

THE ROMAN EMPIRE: THE ROMAN PROVINCES, PROVINCIAL LIFE, THE END OF THE EMPIRE

Imperialism was very much an all-Roman project. There is no evidence of there having been any kind of serious anti-imperial discourse in the city at any time or any real opposition to the rolling sequence of conquests that led to the formation of the empire. Some kind of a discourse around the *idea* of imperialism, though, is suggested in the writings of the historian Tacitus when he is describing the parading in Rome of the defeated anti-Roman Briton Caratacus and his freeing by the senate after a noble address to them on the very nature of Roman power. Subsequently looking around and taking in the sheer grandeur of the city, Caratacus makes his famous observation, or rather Tacitus questions the imperial programme through the words that he has placed in Caratacus's mouth: 'Why, then, do you who have such possessions and so many of them covet our poor huts?'

THE EMPIRE

The empire reached its greatest expanse under the emperor Trajan. A period of retrenchment and reassessment followed almost immediately after Trajan's death in AD 117 during the reign of his successor Hadrian. Not only did Hadrian almost symbolically beat the bounds of the empire with an extended series of visits to the provinces, but he also devised the delineation of frontier defences in a number of provinces, most famously in Britain with the building of what we now call Hadrian's Wall.

What made the huge empire governable was the Roman road network, initially conceived as part of the military infrastructure necessary to control Italy and the provinces by allowing rapid and unimpeded movement of troops from one point to another. Over 250,000 miles of paved or cobbled roads, forts and fortresses, and official staging posts served both the military and the bureaucrats and civil servants travelling on official business. The system also made it more convenient to track and transport goods and levy taxes on their trade if appropriate. Official

Above: Personification of the province of Gaul, Temple of the Divine Hadrian, Rome. (Capitoline Museums, Rome)

Below: A stretch of the ancient Via Appia just outside of Rome.

digests or gazetteers such as the *Antonine Itinerary* listed the main towns in each province and the distance by road between them in a way that would have helped the reader to construct mental maps if not planning an actual journey and to conceptualise the vastness of the empire.

Life in the Roman provinces was characterised by the adoption of certain elements of a common Roman or Romanised material culture by the local elites and later by others further down the social hierarchy. Mosaics and bathhouses are almost *the* defining items of Roman elite culture. While this led to a certain degree of similarity between provinces, local differences were much more marked in the way that this adoption took place and in the manner in which this was expressed. We know that armed resistance to Roman forces was considerable before the initial establishment of certain provinces and that revolts or uprisings against Roman rule also occurred, most notably in Judaea and Britain. Rather than being a unified, smooth process it would appear that throughout the empire Roman imperialism was experienced in different ways by different people at different times. In other words, there would have been many discrepant experiences of conquest and assimilation.

The Roman system implicitly relied on faith in the transformation of conquered peoples into citizens of the empire. Certain parts of the empire do appear to have been viewed particularly favourably by the Romans, most notably Greece for cultural reasons and Egypt both by reason of its huge importance in supplying grain to Rome and the grip that its allegedly exotic nature had on the Roman imagination.

Personification possibly of the province of Mauretania, Temple of the Divine Hadrian, Rome. (Capitoline Museums, Rome)

The question must be asked as to whether there was racial prejudice in the Roman world. A simple yes or no answer is impossible to give, as evidence can be shaped to support positive views of Rome's cosmopolitan nature in addition to neutral views and negative ones. If Athenaeus could write admiringly about Rome being 'the epitome of the world', with peoples from all the cities of the empire resident there to its benefit, then Juvenal could have his fictional character Umbricius rail against some of the same foreign residents: 'I cannot bear ... the city being Greek. But what proportion of the scum is really Greek? For a long time the Syrian Orontes has poured into the Tiber.' Snide comments might have been made about Gauls in the senate but whatever overt prejudice there might have been was never recorded as leading to anything resembling racial violence or pogroms which could potentially have occurred given the stark differences in power that existed between the Roman state and the conquered peoples of its empire and the peoples of the lands beyond its frontiers. The burning of German villages and relentlessly savage violence of the Roman army against both enemy barbarian soldiers and barbarian civilians, including women and children, depicted in images on the helical frieze around the Column of Marcus Aurelius in Rome represented the terrible and harsh realities of ancient warfare rather than ethnic cleansing as we understand that term today.

The Column of Marcus Aurelius, Rome.

ROMAN BRITAIN

As an example of a Roman province we can look at Britain, the province of *Britannia* brought into the Roman Empire by military invasion in AD 43 by the emperor Claudius, almost a hundred years after Julius Caesar's exploratory expeditions to Britain in 55 and 54 BC. While Claudius may have taken credit for the conquest of the country and its annexation as a province, it would in fact be many years before any semblance of a pacified land existed. Claudius's conquered territory consisted mainly of south-eastern England, along with parts of East Anglia and the Midlands. The precarious nature of the early Roman occupation can be assumed from the state of crisis brought about by the Boudiccan uprising in Britain in AD 60.

As was the case with any new province, it is likely that the Roman state quickly cashed in on the assets of the conquered territory through the collection and transportation of slaves, the shipping of war booty to Rome, the location, development and exploitation of local mineral deposits such as gold, silver, lead, tin, bronze and iron, quarrying, agricultural bounty principally in the form of grain, and then by continuing regular taxation. Many of the province's young men were now also recruited into the Roman army in large numbers to serve abroad.

The Roman authorities utilised the pre-existing, pre-Roman Iron Age tribal system in their organisation of the regional cantons, or *civitates,* of the province as they did throughout the empire. This allowed the tribal elites to retain some degree of power through their cooperation in the system.

A considerable force of the Roman army remained stationed in Britain throughout most of the life of the province, mainly in the northern militarised zone. Formal frontiers were established under Hadrian and Antoninus Pius and the frontier works known as Hadrian's Wall in northern England and the Antonine Wall in Scotland acted both as defensive barriers and trade and taxation points.

Urbanisation in the province was rapid, though patchy, and some towns were more successful than others. A number of veteran colonies or *coloniae* were established, initially as further security measures against civil unrest and as demonstrations of urban living to the indigenous population.

In the countryside, Roman-style villas were built by some members of the tribal elite, though the agricultural economy was always dominated by small farmsteads of one kind or another. An agricultural revolution occurred in the later centuries of Roman rule rather than at the beginning as might have been imagined. Roman goods were acquired initially by the elite to enhance their status, though this process soon filtered down the social hierarchy; however, even

Hadrian's Wall, Britain.

towards the end of the fourth century there were still parts of Britain resistant to the lure of Romanised goods, particularly in the more remote countryside, where subsistence agriculture was still practised by necessity. The Roman historian Tacitus tells us that under the governorship of his father-in-law, Gnaeus Julius Agricola in AD 77–85, 'with private encouragement and official aid he pressed forward the building of temples, forums and townhouses … The sons of leading men were schooled in the arts … the refusal to learn Latin was replaced by a desire to excel in it and in the same way Roman dress came into fashion and the toga was worn everywhere.'

Few Britons would ever have travelled outside the province, unless serving as soldiers or working as merchants or in shipping, and certainly not to Rome; we only have three inscribed funerary monuments of Britons who died there. Few serving Roman emperors ever set foot in Britain, among that number being Claudius, Hadrian, Septimius Severus and Constantius Chlorus, who died at York, where his son Constantine was then proclaimed emperor by his troops in AD 306. Vespasian served in the military in Britain before becoming emperor.

The ending of Roman Britain, when it came in AD 410, did not appear to have been altogether a surprise. Some of the province's elite had chosen to try for secession from the central Roman state by throwing their support behind the usurpers Carausius and Allectus at the very end of the third century AD, when to all intents and purposes Britain was autonomous. Even though brought back into the empire by force of Roman arms, the experience of going it alone had not perhaps been as traumatic as many had imagined; indeed, life went on much as before and taxes were still collected, just by a different authority. Pressure on the northern frontier in Britain, raids across the Irish Sea and particularly across the English Channel into the rich south-eastern parts of the province in the later third century and throughout the fourth helped destabilise the province in the same way that barbarian incursions across the frontiers were doing elsewhere in the empire. That the authorities in Rome washed their hands of the province of Britain and told it to look to its own defence in AD 410 made great sense in military terms at the time.

To some extent it is true to say that Roman culture in Britain was simply a veneer. Where most ingrained, that is among the province's elite, this was simply because it was in their interests to adopt Roman ways in order to be allowed to retain some degree of power and authority. In the archaeological record we can see the sloughing off of Romanised material culture that had held sway for 367 years as a surprisingly easy and rapid process after AD 410.

We have no idea at all what an ordinary Briton thought about being a subject of the Roman Empire, nor do we have any views on this matter from the Roman side. However, some clue to the nature of the relationship might be found in one of the famous Vindolanda letters on a preserved wooden writing tablet from a military fort in northern England, in which a Roman office dismissively refers to the local population as '*Brittunculi*' – 'the wretched little Brits'.

THE END OF THE WESTERN EMPIRE

It is now recognised that there was no straightforward decline and fall of the Roman Empire, and certainly not one brought about by barbarian invasions as such. Rather, a whole series of factors appears to have come together to precipitate the gradual collapse of the state and its political, military and bureaucratic machinery from the third century AD onwards. Into this mix must be factored the impact of climate change, environmental damage, agricultural failures, population movement on a colossal scale, a crisis in the management of fear, competing visions of empire within the Roman world and a resistance to necessary change. The deliberately conceived permeability of the frontiers of the Roman Empire, which had done so much to facilitate trade and exchange, now aggravated their vulnerability and contributed towards the gradually evolving crisis. Again, the pragmatic Roman policy of dealing directly with local barbarian leaders both on the fringes of the empire and outside it led to an increase in the individual power of such men and to growing social hierarchies and confederation among various barbarian peoples. In other words, Roman policy actively, but accidentally, contributed towards the emergence of the kind of strong barbarian leaders like Alaric, Athulf and Attila who would eventually so endanger the Roman way of life itself.

At some stage it became official Roman policy to resettle certain groups of barbarian peoples on land within the borders of the empire and to rely increasingly on such people to join up to serve in the Roman army in the same way that centuries before newly conquered provincials had been conscripted to serve Rome. The growing barbarianisation of the army also led to the growing power of the leaders of these barbarian forces. This is well illustrated by the life of the general Stilicho, half-Roman on his mother's side and half-Vandal on his father's. Such a lineage allowed him to attain almost unprecedented personal levels of power in Rome and in the army of the Western Roman Empire and he became quite literally the feared power behind the throne of the emperor Honorius in the first decade of his reign. Stilicho's arrest and execution at Ravenna in AD 408 demonstrated how many enemies he had acquired along the way.

There were large numbers of severe violent incursions into Roman territories by barbarian war bands, increased activity by pirates and coastal raids in Britain and Gaul in the third and fourth centuries AD, but these did not constitute any kind of coordinated military threat. It was just a large number of isolated incidents, occurring again and again and again. It was 'like a river that has burst its banks', as one contemporary commentator so evocatively wrote. These minor incursions just went on and on, particular pressure being felt from the Saxons and Franks on the lower and middle Rhine frontier and from the Goths on the lower Danube, who themselves were under pressure from the Huns moving off the Russian steppes. The raiders were hard to track down and kill. They were said to be 'like ghosts instead of men', so easily could they hide out among the local frontier populations, many of whom were of the same tribal groups in any case. With the total length of the Roman frontiers being almost 5000 miles, protecting every part of the empire from incursions proved impossible.

When there were larger-scale clashes such events must have sent shock waves through Roman provincial society and impacted greatly on the people of Rome itself, whose vulnerability had not been so starkly exposed since the time of

Battles with barbarians on the Ludovisi Sarcophagus. (National Roman Museum, Rome)

Hannibal. At the Battle of Strasbourg, also known as the Battle of Argentoratum, in AD 357 the emperor Julian easily saw off a confederate force of Alemanni led by Chnodomar and drove the stricken remnants of the group back across the Rhine. Roman casualties were reported as being only 243 dead, suggesting that this was a minor, though not insignificant, clash of arms. However, in AD 378 the emperor Valens was slain at the Battle of Adrianople in Thrace in modern-day Turkey and his army routed by a Goth army led by Fritigern.

It is not possible to say exactly when the Western Roman Empire fell in the way that we can accurately date the fall of the Soviet Union in our own times, as it was such a prolonged process involving change and transition rather than sudden, violent schism. The single monolithic state had simply already split into numerous successor states by the end. However, there are certain key events, separated by almost a hundred years, that together can be thought of as constituting the end of the Roman Empire. On the night of 31 December AD 406, sizeable forces of Vandals, Alans and Suebi crossed the frozen Rhine into Roman territory, over a number of years sacking towns and settlements in the provinces of Gaul, Spain and north Africa almost without serious resistance from the overstretched central authority in Rome. Totally unconnected to these events was the manoeuvring of Alaric and his Visigoths, who moved into Greece and thence to Italy, where they laid siege to Milan, were defeated, regrouped and then blockaded Rome, taking and sacking the city in AD 410. The Visigoths did not occupy the city but moved on to Sicily, eventually negotiating with the Roman imperial authorities for their resettlement within the empire in Aquitaine. It is no wonder that the central Roman authorities told the Britons to look to their own defence in AD 410.

Yet, after all this, the Romans managed to fight back and indeed retain control, if not full authority, over the remaining provinces of the empire in the west. In AD 439 the Vandals captured Carthage and to all intents and purposes put an end to the existence of the Roman north African provinces, severing trade routes and curtailing the collection of taxes and grain supplies. The unification of the Huns under Attila in AD 444 marked a serious enhancement of the danger to the Eastern Roman Empire and it was only a matter of time before he turned his attention to the already weakened and beleaguered Roman authority in the Western Roman Empire. Invading Gaul in 451 but being repulsed by forces under Aetius, he regrouped and entered Italy the next year to march on Rome. Circumstances conspired against him and no attack on the city took place. Attila died in 453. In 454 the Vandals, now an even more powerful force, sailed to Italy and sacked Rome, the second time the city had seen its once indomitable security breached by barbarian forces in the space of forty years or so. In 468 the combined armies of the western and eastern Roman Empires mounted an expedition to retake the former north African provinces occupied by the Vandals, a mission that ended in disaster and defeat for the Romans. In AD 476, on 4 September, Odoacer deposed the Western Roman Emperor Romulus Augustulus, an event tinged with a certain amount of irony in that the last emperor's name was also that of its legendary founder, and symbolically despatched the imperial insignia of Rome to Constantinople. Many historians see this as the final act in the drama of our story of ancient Rome, while others would place this event much earlier. Others still would claim to see the continuance of Roman structures of power in some parts of the Western Roman Empire and of a unified, centralised authority in control of the city of Rome itself.

6

EVERYDAY LIFE IN ANCIENT ROME

The Daily Round

The daily routine of Rome's citizens would very much have depended on where in the social hierarchy any particular individual belonged, and on top of that whether we are talking about the daily life of a man or of a woman. Many women of the middling or richer sort were very much tied to their *domus*, or home, by male-imposed tradition. For slaves and for those citizens at the very base of the hierarchy, life would have been regimented, probably a regime of repetitive jobs or tasks to be performed day in and day out. For those in the middle and upper echelons of the social hierarchy, life would have been more comfortable and much less predictable.

At the Baths, in the Forum, at the Library

For many men a visit to the public baths would have provided an opportunity not just for keeping hygienically clean and physically fit but also for socialising with friends or even conducting business. There may have been as many as nine hundred such establishments in Rome by the fourth century AD.

Seneca the Younger, writing in the AD 60s, bemoans the volume of noise coming from the nearby baths: the groans of exercising men, the insistent slap of the masseur's hands on his client's body, the delighted shouts of the victorious ball players, the loud splash of bathers jumping into the plunge baths, the hubbub surrounding the apprehension of a thief, the yelling of people having their hair plucked, and the cries of the sausage seller, the fast food cooks, and the confectioner as they hawk their wares to the hungry bathers.

Above and below: The Baths of Caracalla, Rome.

Some time in the day might be spent in the Forum, or rather in one of the many fora that Rome had been provided with by the middle imperial era. The original *Forum Romanum*, simply a large, open public space, represented at the time the commercial and political epicentre of the city and here business would be conducted, political meetings and debates held, legal business and trials carried out, religious rites practised, public feasts and funerals observed. As market and trading activities moved away to large, specialised fora, so the first forum came to be encroached upon by temples, monuments and statues to the great and good of contemporary Rome and of its glorious past, making it a cultural and religious centre as much as a political and legal one.

For the literate Roman, leisure time could also pleasurably and usefully be spent in the reading of books, either in a private library in the reader's home or in one of the city's public libraries founded during the empire or in the collections at the larger public baths. Access to the city's most significant book collections in the imperial libraries would, of course, have been restricted. Books at the time took the form of either rolled scrolls of paper, vellum, papyrus or other similar material or, later, a codex arrangement of such leaves that was the forerunner of the modern book, this latter format becoming pre-eminent by the early fourth century AD. Book dealers employing teams of scribes to copy manuscripts in Latin or Greek would have existed to satisfy the market for both poetry and prose of all kinds, from epic and tragedy to comedy, and for titles in the fields of history, science, medicine, rhetoric and philosophy. It is known that huge quantities of Greek books were brought to Rome at the height of the Republic as war booty from conquests in the eastern Mediterranean, as indeed at the same time were thousands of Greek statues and other works of art. Roman imperialism was not always necessarily simply a matter of the acquisition of more apparently valuable booty such as gold and silver items, slaves, taxes and mineral exploitation rights.

Letter writing between elite friends would also appear to have been popular, the most famous such surviving correspondence being the highly polished and published letters sent by the Republican statesman and lawyer Cicero to his friend Atticus. The material paraphernalia for writing letters – pens and styli, inkpots and decorated gemstone seals – are found regularly in archaeological excavations in Rome and in the provinces.

THE GAMES AND THE THEATRE

When the Roman poet Juvenal complained about the political apathy of his fellow citizens of the late first and early second century AD when faced with autocratic emperors, he coined a famous phrase that would resound down the years. These citizens craved and were satisfied with '*panem et circenses*', that is 'bread and circuses', he wrote. Many emperors found that the provision of mass entertainment and the occasional public distribution of free grain easily diverted critical attention away from the more negative aspects of their reigns. The provision of such spectacles was a necessary strategy for making imperial power visible in Rome.

It was in the Colosseum in Rome that regular shameful bloody spectacles in the guise of entertainment were played out to baying crowds of anywhere between 50,000 and 80,000 people. These took the form of public executions, gladiatorial

The Colosseum, Rome.

The Colosseum, Rome.

Gladiatorial combat. (Archaelogical Museum, Bologna)

games, *venatios* or wild beast hunts, and mock naval battles. Inaugurated in AD 80 in the reign of the emperor Titus, the building continued in use for gladiatorial shows until around AD 435 and for animal hunts up to the AD 520s.

At the inaugural games in the Colosseum, the poet Martial tells us that one of the highlights was the combat between the two gladiators Priscus, possibly a Gaul, and Verus. Their fight was so long and enthralling, with neither man being able to get the better of the other, though not through want of trying, that the sympathetic catcalling and cheering of the audience spurred Titus on to have both men awarded palm branches and small symbolic wooden swords that usually were given to gladiators to mark their retirement, if they had survived that long in this perilous career. Thus both men walked alive and free from the arena on that day to the cheers of the crowd and the plaudits of those in the imperial box.

Gladiatorial combat. Cast from a funerary monument. Colosseum, Rome.

At the same inaugural games, a stand-out performance was also recorded from the *bestiarius* or beast-fighter Carpophores, who slew a bear, a lion and a leopard in a single battle. On another occasion he is said to have killed twenty animals, including a rhinoceros, which he despatched with a spear, leading to his acclamation by the crowd as the new Hercules. Another good illustration of the almost stupefying scale of slaughter in the arena is provided by the records relating to celebratory games put on for the Roman people by the emperor Trajan over several months with monies accrued from his bloody conquest of Dacia in AD 107: 10,000 gladiators fought and 11,000 large animals were killed in the *venationes*. Animals as diverse as African elephants and lions, Indian tigers and Dalmatian bears would have evoked wonder in the spectators' eyes, even without the spectacle of their needless butchering for further entertainment. A whole industry, probably employing thousands of people, would have been in existence simply geared towards the hunting, trapping and capture of such beasts in their natural environments, their shipping overseas to Rome by both land and sea, and their tending and feeding while in transit and at the Colosseum prior to their killing in the name of culture.

Gladiators were almost mythic characters, hyper-masculine figures who appealed as much to women as to men. Although there are historical references

Mosaic of animals being prepared to fight in the arena. Colosseum, Rome.

in Roman writings to female gladiators, and a marble relief recording the freeing of a pair of female fighters called Amazon and Achilia has been found at Halicarnassus in modern Turkey, the vast majority of gladiators were men, and foreign men at that. They came to gladiatorial training schools as captives from Roman conquests or as condemned criminals. Curiously, though, it would appear that gladiatorial contests had not always been public entertainments as they became; indeed, it is thought that the very first gladiatorial contest was an event put on at an aristocratic funeral in 264 BC to honour the power and status of the deceased, therefore imbuing the fight with a ritual significance and purpose.

The Circus Maximus, Rome.

Circus racing on a relief from Ostia. (Vatican Museums, Rome).

A short distance away from the Colosseum, chariot racing took place at the Circus Maximus, the elongated track that filled the valley between the Palatine and Aventine hills and which could accommodate a potential audience of around 250,000 people. Here the people could watch the races between the teams from the four great Roman stables, identified by their colours as the blues, greens, reds and whites, and cheer on celebrity charioteers such as Diocles, who over a twenty-four-year career drove in 4,257 races and won 1,462 times.

Public entertainment was not always so vicarious a thrill as a day watching combat at the Colosseum or at the chariot races, and the theatre sometimes provided more cerebral nourishment for the Romans in the form of both crude street theatre and mime and more traditional plays by popular Roman playwrights, such as Plautus and Terence, staged in Rome's three purpose-built theatre buildings. Much of the theatre repertoire consisted of Greek plays, and indeed most of the actors in both the Greek and Roman plays would have been ethnic Greeks. While both men and women might have appeared in street mimes, on stage the cadre of professional actors would all have been men, donning women's clothes and wearing masks when required to play female characters. The most important and best-surviving of Rome's theatres was the Theatre of Marcellus, planned by Julius Caesar but completed during the reign of Augustus. Sited near the Circus Flaminius

The Theatre of Marcellus, Rome.

at the foot of the Capitoline Hill, this massive building could house up to 20,000 people on its semi-circular banks of tiered seating.

EATING AND DRINKING

The Roman diet would again have varied greatly according to social class. It is unlikely that anyone rich actually would ever have eaten the outlandish dishes of dormice sprinkled with poppy seeds and drizzled with honey, or live birds stitched up inside a cooked pig's carcass as served at Trimalchio's feast in Petronius's biting Neronian satire on the foibles and pretensions of this fictional but symbolic millionaire freedman. Equally, although a fourth- or fifth-century AD Roman cookbook by Apicius has come down to us, it is unlikely to provide anything other than a guide to food consumed perhaps by only the very wealthiest people of the day, or food that was fashionable and faddish at that time.

Shopping at the city's many bustling markets would have taken up much of the early part of the day for those whose job or duty it was to cook for their household or master and mistress. A slave attempting to fulfil his or her master's orders for the day might have had to run numerous errands, for instance buying bread from a bakery such as that owned by Marcus Vergilius Eurysaces and meat from a pork butcher like Tiberius Julius Vitalis before returning home via the Porta Fontinalis on the Capitoline Hill to collect some new shoes for the master from the premises of the cobbler and shoemaker Gaius Julius Helius. These three named Roman tradesmen and businessmen were indeed real people, commemorated on funerary monuments in the city, though not actually contemporaries, as I have suggested here for purely illustrative purposes.

The basis of the diet probably consumed by most Romans would have been cereals such as wheat and barley, commonly made into bread and cakes, dried pulses, particularly broad beans and lentils, fresh vegetables and fruit, especially apples, pears, plums, berries of various kinds, grapes and figs, nuts such as hazelnuts, pine nuts, walnuts, almonds and imported pistachios, dried seeds such as watermelon, and occasionally meat, game and fish if the diner was rich enough. Herbs such as oregano, rosemary, fennel, purslane and bay were commonly used to enhance flavour, as were capers and citrus fruits of some kind, perhaps citrons rather than lemons as such. Food routinely would have been seasoned with salt, sometimes with the more exotic and expensive white and black peppers or other traded spices, or smothered in robust sauces like the famous *garum*, a potent fermented fish sauce. Olive oil would have been used for cooking and wine or beer would have been drunk with the meal. Vegetables such as tomatoes, peppers, and aubergines, which we think of today as being quintessentially Italian, are relatively modern introductions. It is likely that Rome's foreign residents tried to adhere to their own traditional ethnic foodways if the relevant produce to do so was available to them.

Family Life

Throughout its history a great deal of importance was placed on marriage and on the Roman family and the very concept of a harmonious family life underpinning the harmonious workings of the state. In the early Republican period the veneration of the ancestors was prevalent among the most aristocratic Roman families, establishing family lineage being a way of asserting hereditary power. Such families would have possessed and curated images of their ancestors – known as *imagines* – in the form of wax masks which would be kept displayed in their homes for most of the time but which would be brought out at funerals to be worn by family members, thus symbolically bringing their ancestors back to life. Later, the practice extended further down the social hierarchy and the wax mask images were replaced by statuary busts and heads, suggesting perhaps that the art of Roman portraiture owed its origins to the creation of these wax ancestral masks.

The very conservative nature of Roman society might appear to us today to be very stifling, with women ostensibly taking on the exclusive roles of wives or mothers and being confined to the home, but occasionally archaeological discoveries allow us glimpses of other, less traditional and sometimes perhaps surprising aspects of the culture, as in the case of the working women already discussed elsewhere in this book. Again, while museums in Rome and elsewhere have extensive collections of ancient Roman funerary monuments commemorating married couples and families presented as the norm in that society, a memorial in the collections of the British Museum hints at the existence of alternative lifestyles for some individuals.

The marble window funerary relief of Fonteia Eleusis and Fonteia Helena, both described in the accompanying inscription as being freedwomen of Gaia Fonteia, probably dates to the Augustan period, that is the late first century BC or the early first century AD. The depiction of the two women together marks this funerary monument out as unusual, in that they hold their right hands clasped together in a gesture which normally was used in Roman art to symbolise a married couple. The heads of both women are turned towards each other and some time later the head and face of the left-hand woman has been re-carved to become that of a man. The motive for re-cutting and in the process reconfiguring the relief and its meaning must remain unknown. However, it is generally accepted that the Fonteii funerary image did indeed represent the celebration and commemoration of a same-sex female relationship.

Visiting the Doctor

Like anyone, the Romans would on occasion fall sick or have to visit a doctor. Most doctors in the Roman world were men and ethnic Greeks, though some exceptions are known. We know something of the medicines and natural remedies doled out to patients on such occasions from contemporary writers. Archaeological finds of doctor's equipment and instruments provide further insight into medical practice. Items such as occulists' stamps for marking eye ointments are surprisingly common finds. Cupping vessels for collecting blood, and surgical tools such as scalpels, knives, probes, forceps and saws attest to surgical practices which without modern anaesthetics and sophisticated follow-up care probably led to death more often than they helped to preserve life. Without money to pay medical bills or easy access to a doctor's services, often the sick would have no alternative but to rely on folk medicine and superstitious practices or to simply place themselves in the hands of the gods, especially Aesculapius or Hygeia, in seeking a cure either through prayer and gift-giving or by visiting a temple or specialised healing shrine.

7

RELIGION, DEATH AND BURIAL: PAGANS AND CHRISTIANS

PAGAN GODS

Roman religion was a highly complex amalgam of Romanised Greek deities and beliefs and Italic and native Roman rites and ritual traditions. The Roman pantheon of gods was headed up by the Capitoline Triad of Jupiter, Juno and Minerva, worshipped in their magnificent temple on the Capitoline Hill in the heart of Rome and at smaller temples throughout the city. These all-powerful gods were of particular importance to Rome's wealthier citizens. The city's plebeian population was more favourable towards another triad of deities whose members, Ceres, Liber and Libera, were all associated with agricultural and human fertility and with the overseeing of rites of passage into adulthood. Their temple was on the Aventine Hill. Also of great significance in political terms was the imperial cult, which had a particular appeal in the Greek east of the empire.

Other well-known Roman deities included Mercury, god of travel and commerce, Venus, the goddess of love and female beauty with whom women would particularly have identified, and Bacchus, god of wine and agricultural bounty. Another goddess linked with Rome's deep past was Vesta, the Roman goddess of the hearth, and thus of the *domus* or home, that hugely important symbolic centre of Roman social structures. Her small, round temple in the Roman Forum housed a sacred flame that represented the hearth of the city itself. Each year this fire would be rekindled and otherwise would be tended throughout the year by the Vestal Virgins, the six priestesses of the cult. This linking of the cult of Vesta with the very origins of Rome and thus with its highly potent foundation myths was further emphasised by the Vestal Virgins' curation of a statue of Athena said to have been rescued from Troy by Aeneas and small statues of guardian deities. These were kept in secure storage in a cult storehouse, access to which was restricted, although once a year at the festival of the *Vestalia* it was opened to married women who walked in bare-footed procession through the building and left food offerings which they had brought with them. Later in the same week the storehouse was ritually cleansed and the offerings taken to the River Tiber for formal disposal. The college of the Vestal Virgins was disbanded in AD 394 and the sacred flame then extinguished.

The Temple of Vesta, Rome.

The priestesses were chosen at a young age by lot and groomed for the role before induction. Over the years a number of female members of the imperial house became Vestals, indicating the importance of the cult. That women had to renounce their natural sexuality and forego marriage at the traditional age to fulfil the role is curious, in that chastity in a woman and favouring the single state would appear to have been diametrically opposed to the idea that the greatest virtues that a Roman woman possessed were related to marriage and motherhood. Stranger still perhaps was the fact that the Vestal Virgins each served thirty years in the role before stepping down to allow a younger Virgin to take their place and then were permitted to marry. A man who married an ex-Vestal gained a great deal of social cachet by doing so.

Above: The Pantheon, Rome.

Below: The Temple of Antoninus and Faustina, the Forum, Rome.

The Temple of Portunus, Rome.

The various attributes of different gods allowed individuals to identify with a plethora of deities throughout their lives, depending on the particular circumstances in which they found themselves at any particular time. Were they seeking help to find romance? Were they about to go on a journey? Were they sick? The latter question could most easily be addressed, as all the gods were connected to healing in some way. Hundreds of temples to different deities could be found throughout the city, especially in its centre.

As well as their own gods the Romans also adopted a number of foreign and exotic deities such as Cybele, also known as the *Magna Mater* or Great Mother, and Isis from Egypt. From the second century AD onwards the so-called eastern Mystery Religions, such as Mithraism, appealed because of their exclusivity achieved through often bizarre initiation ceremonies, but principally they offered the hope of salvation. In the provinces Roman imperialism was as much about the syncretism of local deities – the equating of a local god with another, pre-existing Roman one – as it was about the exercise of military might.

In this veritable world of gods people had a choice, as long as they adhered to the established rituals and traditions associated with both public worship

The Round
Temple (of
Hercules Victor),
Rome.

and private rites. A religious calendar of festivals determined the very rhythm
of the Roman year. Public ceremonies, often overseen by the emperor in his role
as *Pontifex Maximus* or chief priest, provided a forum for honouring the great
gods such as the Capitoline Triad, while private worship was more tied in to
veneration of the household gods known as the *penates* or to the honouring of
the *Genius* or guardian spirit of a particular place.

Blood sacrifice lay at the heart of Roman religion, along with the giving of
other gifts to the gods and the vow. Worshippers would sponsor an animal
sacrifice in order to ask the gods for help in some way, or to thank the gods for
having received help, or simply to honour the god and prolong good fortune.

Scene of sacrifice
on the base of
the Decennalia
Monument, the
Forum, Rome.

CHRISTIANITY

However, this pragmatic and seemingly benign view of other religions did not apply when Rome was faced with belief systems that challenged its own world view and threatened its primacy. Thus in Britain and Gaul the local but highly politicised Druidism was repressed. More significantly, in the first and second centuries AD Rome clashed with the Jews, a people whose jealous god would brook no rivals, and with Christians who were thought to be challenging the very

Above: A Christian sarcophagus. (Vatican Museums, Rome)

Right: Statue of the Christian Good Shepherd, from the catacombs on Domitilla. (Vatican Museums, Rome)

authority of the state itself between the reign of Nero in the first century AD and that of Constantine in the fourth. As imperial authority and leadership weakened in the fifth century, so the Christian church seemed to provide alternative structures for the exercising and maintenance of power, increasing its appeal to the elite of Rome and her empire.

It would appear that Christians were present among the population of Rome from at least the time of Nero and indeed the emperor cunningly sought to make members of this community scapegoats for the setting of the great fire that consumed a number of districts of the city in his reign, though this was not organised persecution as such. Trajan's attitude that Christians were criminals who should not be actively sought out but who could be challenged for their beliefs if necessary led to sporadic and occasional local events of persecution and sometimes bloody martyrdom on a small scale over the next 130 years or so. However, during the reign of the emperor Decius (AD 249–251), active persecution of Christians as part of a pagan revitalisation movement became imperial policy. A number of subsequent emperors followed suit, but for somewhat different reasons, culminating in the most sustained campaign of persecution yet seen beginning under Diocletian in AD 303 and over-enthusiastically pursued in particular by Galerius, who died in AD 311. Christians at Rome and in the cities of the empire were now more numerous, visibly more active and more powerful than they had ever been; their church was well organised and well funded, providing almost an alternative state in which Christians could exist. It was this situation which provoked the official persecution and which perversely allowed the church to grow stronger still through its opposition to this state of hysteria and by the blood of its martyrs.

The Diocletianic persecution marked the tipping point in relations between the Roman state and the Christian church. As Constantine swept to power by defeating Maxentius, whom he styled a usurper, at the Battle of the Milvian Bridge and marched into Rome, his triumphal entry was accompanied by stories of his 'Christian vision' on the eve of the battle. Constantine was nothing if not pragmatic – had he not already previously claimed to have seen a 'pagan vision' of Apollo before an earlier victory? He shrewdly understood which way power at Rome was flowing and felt that he could do business with the city's Christian community without confronting them. Despite throwing himself into the sponsoring of church-building in Rome and issuing the ground-breaking Edict of Milan in AD 313, a statement of religious toleration, it was not until he lay on his deathbed in Nicomedia in AD 337 that he finally converted to Christianity. Again, his powerful and influential mother Helena became renowned for her commitment to church-building in Rome and elsewhere and mostly singularly travelled around the Holy Land searching for pieces of the True Cross and other holy Christian relics to bring back to Rome for display and veneration.

It was following the initiative of Constantine that Rome was eventually transformed from a pagan city to a Christian one, with the physical centre of power moving away from the Forum to the more peripheral areas of the Lateran and subsequently the Vatican.

RELIGIOUS FESTIVALS

The origins of many of the religious festivals celebrated annually in Rome probably lay far back in the city's past, and it is likely that though their full meaning might have been lost to many of the revellers on these occasions they nevertheless continued to be celebrated almost in the manner of heritage folk events. Three of those festivals, the *Lupercalia*, the *Cerealia* and the *Saturnalia*, will be considered briefly here. The *Lupercalia* was celebrated each year on 14 February. On this occasion young men, mainly from the upper classes of Roman society, ran through the streets naked, striking watchers and bystanders with a goatskin thong which hung from the end of a short stick. Many women in the crowds would openly and freely proffer their hands for striking in the hope that this action would somehow help them to become pregnant, particularly those who had already had problems in conceiving naturally. The significance of this event in the Roman calendar can be gauged from the fact that in 44 BC one of the naked running 'wolf men' – the *Luperci* – was none other than Mark Antony. The *Cerealia* festival was held over seven days in mid to late April, and as the name implies was dedicated to the celebration of Ceres, the goddess of grain, agricultural fertility and, by association, human fertility. One of the most bizarre elements of this celebration involved, according to the Roman poet Ovid, live foxes being released into the Circus Maximus with burning torches tied to their tails, the poor creatures then suffering a terrible end by being burned to death as they publicly struggled to shake off the torches. White-clad young girls carrying torches would also re-enact the search for Ceres's abducted daughter Proserpina, who had been carried off by Hades to the underworld and raped and imprisoned there.

The *Saturnalia* festival took place each year on 17 December, the festival later being extended to 23 December. Ostensibly dedicated to celebrating the Italic god Saturnus, the emphasis of the rites would appear to have been personal and spiritual liberation and the acceptance of a world turned temporarily upside down. A mock king oversaw festivities and the social classes mixed in a way that would not have occurred ordinarily. Regulations and conventions pertaining to slaves were allowed to lapse over the course of the festival, and a false freedom was allowed them, of course with certain boundaries still in place and not to be crossed. Feasting, drinking, carousing and the exchange of gifts such as pottery figurines and wax candles were the order of the day. Riotous or licentious behaviour would not necessarily be frowned upon at this time. Normal dress codes were ignored by all.

Such pagan festivals were celebrated well into the late Roman period and in some cases into the formally Christian era; people would still take the opportunity to party on these occasions like it was AD 99.

In addition to more organised religious practices, there was also a considerable folk religion that to all intents and purposes constituted a body of superstitions. Very serious attention was paid to the pronouncements of augurs, who would determine omens from observing the flight of birds, or *haruspices*, who would examine the entrails and livers of sacrificial birds and animals for signs.

Tomb of the Platorini, reconstructed in the National Roman Museum, Rome.

FUNERARY COMMEMORATION AND THE AFTERLIFE

The Roman belief in some kind of afterlife is reflected in the sheer importance of funerary commemoration in Roman society and in the funerary monuments constructed on the main roads such as the Via Appia leading out of the city. Cremation of the body was the principal burial rite until the second century AD, when it was generally replaced by inhumation burial, though cremation remained the preferred rite of some higher-status individuals. Commonly, excavated inhumation burials have a coin placed in the mouth of the buried body to allow its soul to pay Charon, the mythical ferryman, to carry the body across the River Styx to Hades, the underworld.

Of Rome's thousands of funerary monuments, the surviving Tomb of Eurysaces the Baker, Pyramid of Cestius and Tomb of Caecilia Metella represent three of the most unusual and singular monuments set up by Roman private citizens.

The tomb of Marcus Vergilius Eurysaces the Baker, right up against the Porta Maggiore, dates to around 30 BC and takes the form of what is generally interpreted to be a giant bread oven, adorned with an upper frieze relief depicting workers inside his bakery, making, baking and stacking loaves. Eurysaces was probably a highly successful freedman who made a fortune as a bakery contractor.

The Pyramid of Gaius Cestius Epulo, near the Ostia Gate, was built around 12

Below left: The Tomb of Eurysaces the Baker, Rome.

Below right: The Pyramid of Cestius, Rome.

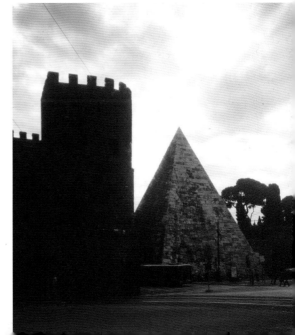

The Tomb of the Hatesri. (Vatican Museum, Rome)

BC and is both an extraordinary survival and a unique monument of its time. It represents a manifestation of the Egyptomania which so gripped Rome during the era of Cleopatra. Built of concrete faced with white luna marble, it stands over 100 feet high. Surprisingly, little is known of Cestius, other than that he served at various times as a praetor and a tribune of the plebs and held a minor religious office.

The tomb of the aristocratic and well-connected Roman woman Caecilia Metella, by the third milestone outside the city on the Via Appia, is a vast tower tomb later incorporated into a medieval fortress. Now sadly stripped of much of its marble facing, it dates to the last quarter of the first century BC. The decorative scheme would appear to have consisted of bull's skulls and garlands and military trophies, reflecting the family's military heritage.

Large portions of a fourth remarkable funerary monument, the Tomb of the Haterii, which once stood on the Via Labicana, are on display today in the Vatican Museums in Rome. Quintus Haterius, a rich freedman in the later first century AD, would appear to have been a highly successful building contractor in the city. His family tomb carried intricate reliefs depicting the lying-in state of his dead

The Tomb of Caecilia Metella, Rome.

wife, images of numerous buildings along the Sacra Via, and of a huge building crane powered by slaves on a wheel caught in the process of constructing a tomb.

EPITAPHS

There are tens of thousands of Roman funerary inscriptions that have come down to us, to be meticulously catalogued and analysed for the information they can give us about the Latin language, about attitudes towards death, about individual lives of both men and women and sometimes children, about population trends such as life expectancy, and about Roman social structures such as marriage, parenthood and friendship. Although it is slightly invidious to have to choose one or two examples from the city of Rome here to illustrate these broader points, given that there are so many to choose from, I have selected the second-century BC epitaphs of a member of the influential Scipio family, inscribed on his sarcophagus; of a woman known to us only as Claudia, her inscribed tablet now lost; and of Marcus Caecilius, commemorated on a stone found on the Appian Way just outside of the city.

The Scipio family inscription reads,

Gnaeus Cornelius Scipio Hispanus, son of Gnaeus, praetor, curule aedile, quaestor, tribune of soldiers (twice), member of the Board of Ten for judging lawsuits, member of the Board of Ten for making sacrifices … By my good conduct I heaped virtues on the virtue of my clan, I begat a family and sought to equal the exploits of my father. I upheld the praise of my ancestors, so that they are glad that I was created of their line. My honours have ennobled my stock.

Claudia's epitaph reads,

Stranger, my message is short. Stop and read it. This is the unlovely tomb of a lovely woman. Her parents gave her the name Claudia. She loved her husband with all her heart. She bore two children, one of whom she left on earth, the other beneath it. She had a pleasing way of talking and walking. She tended the house and worked wool. I have said my piece. Go your way.

Caecilius's epitaph reads,

This memorial was made for Marcus Caecilius. Thank you, my dear guest, for stopping at my abode. Good luck and good health to you. Sleep without a care.

The Scipio epitaph, though the longest of the three selected, perhaps tells us less about the character of the recipient than the other two do, and a great deal about his status and class. The language and content of his epitaph are redolent of themes centred around male achievement, service and duty, family, lineage and the ancestors. Claudia is presented in her epitaph as having taken great pride in her more simple achievements: to have been a nice person, a loving wife and mother, and an efficient household manager, skilled in women's crafts, and thus incidentally morally grounded. Of Marcus Caecilius we learn almost nothing from a reading of his brief epitaph but take away the impression of a pleasant and affable fellow, unconcerned with service, duty, titles and responsibilities.

THE CATACOMBS

There are few tourists to Rome today – with the exception of your claustrophobic author – who do not visit at least one of the city's many ancient catacombs, sprawling underground rock-cut burial chambers and tunnels used by Christians and Jews for the burial of their dead. The phenomenon of digging such underground cemeteries would seem to have started around AD 150 among the Christians, possibly due to a shortage of burial space along the main roads leading out of the city at this time. Over forty main complexes of catacombs are known, with hundreds, and sometimes thousands, of burials in rock-cut niches inside each one. The catacombs were also used for Christian services, perhaps to honour the religion's many martyrs, and many were decorated with wall and ceiling paintings often depicting biblical characters and stories. These were not secret burial sites, nor was the underground aspect of them in any way particularly significant; however, in the eras of persecution it would have allowed Christians to conduct public religious rites out of sight of any violent opponents.

FAREWELL AND GO YOUR WAY

In the space of ninety pages we have gone from examining overground Rome to discussing aspects of the underground city and from retelling the foundation myths of this once pagan place to considering how it would eventually become a Christian city and loom so large in the history of Christianity in Europe.

WHAT NEXT?

FURTHER READING

Beard, Mary, *SPQR. A History of Ancient Rome* (London: Profile Books, 2015)

Carandini, Andrea, *Rome: Day One* (Princeton University Press, 2011)

Claridge, Amanda, *Rome: An Oxford Archaeological Guide* (2nd edn, Oxford University Press, 2010)

Cornell, Tim, *The Beginnings of Rome. Italy and Rome from the Bronze Age to the Punic Wars (c. 1000–264 BC)* (London: Routledge, 1995)

Dowden, Ken, *Religion and the Romans* (Bristol: Bristol Classical Press, 1992)

Ferris, Iain, *The Mirror of Venus: Women in Roman Art* (Stroud: Amberley Publishing, 2015)

Harlow, Mary & Ray Laurence, *Growing Up and Growing Old in Ancient Rome* (London: Routledge, 2002)

Hopkins, Keith & Mary Beard, *The Colosseum* (London: Profile Books, 2005)

Mattingly, David, *Imperialism, Power and Identity: Experiencing the Roman Empire* (Princeton University Press, 2011)

Noy, David, *Foreigners at Rome: Citizens and Strangers* (London: Duckworth, 2000)

Woolf, Greg, *Rome. An Empire's Story* (Oxford University Press, 2012)

WEBSITES OF INTEREST

www.romansociety.org

www.roman-empire.net

www.forumromanum.org

www.vroma.org

www.capitolium.org

INDEX